LIVE IT

2

JERRY AKERS

OWN IT

Beyond the Pitch, Promise and Prospectus:
Making the Cut in the World of Franchise Ownership

LIVE IT

2

OWN IT

Beyond the Pitch, Promise and Prospectus:
Making the Cut in the World of Franchise Ownership

Written by
Dr. Jeffrey A. Kaplan

FINIS
BRIDGE
PUBLISHING

CHICAGO • LOS ANGELES • VANCOUVER

Published in the United States by Finis~Bridge Publishing.

www.FinisBridge.com

Finis~Bridge books are available for bulk purchase at special discounts for use by educational institutions and students. Special editions, including specialized covers, excerpts of existing books, or books with corporate logos, can be created in large quantities for specialized needs.

For information, contact ReaderServices@FinisBridge.com

Library of Congress Catalogue in-Publication Data is available upon request

Jeff Kaplan – 1st ed.

1. Franchise 2. Small Business 3. Entrepreneurship 4. Business & Money

Paperback ISBN: 978-1-956739-00-8

Hardback ISBN: 978-1-956739-01-5

eBook ISBN: 978-1-956739-02-2

Audiobook ISBN: 978-1-956739-03-9

Printed in the United States of America

Edited by Tara Thomas-Gettman & Kelly Fagan

Book layout by Susan Langman

Book cover by Susan Langman, Amber Moore & Kim Leer

Illustrations by Joe Hox

First Edition

To our families at home and at work.

Thank you for your love, dedication and patience.

You amaze daily.

DR. JEFFREY A. KAPLAN

Dr. Kaplan is an internationally recognized business consultant who has worked with many of the Fortune 100 companies. For nearly 30 years Jeff's writing and research efforts have focused on helping people take charge of their personal and professional development and rapidly accelerate the pace and trajectory of their careers. Jeff is the co-founder of LIFTinnovate, a company dedicated to measuring human experience and accelerating transformative outcomes. As host of the *Willing 2 Win* TV, radio and podcast series, Jeff examines these topics and more. His new *Willing 2 Win* book series will be released November 2022 with the first publication. He is the author of *Everybody Sells*, the industry standard for B2B team selling, and contributed to the New York Times bestseller *Who's Got Your Back*.

JERRY AKERS

Sought out by independent businesses from coast-to-coast, Jerry is a frequent keynote speaker and consults for many of the nation's most successful multi-unit franchise operators. Akers brings extensive business experience as a corporate executive and a successful multi-unit, multi-brand franchise operator. A Midwest native, Jerry lives on a family farm in northeast Iowa but enjoys time away at his lake house in central Arkansas. Jerry serves on the International Franchise Association Franchisee Forum Board, National Federation of Independent Business State Leadership Council, Iowa Board of Cosmetology Arts and Sciences and Great Clips Advisory Board.

RESOURCES

Franchising is a life-altering commitment that requires detailed preparation and ongoing execution. That's why we created resources to provide what you need when you need it. *Live It 2 Own It* (L2O) support includes the print, e-book and audio editions of the book and a resource-rich website (www.liveit2ownit.com)—all to help you successfully navigate your franchise journey.

E-Book Edition

Digital availability ensures access to the book on any digital reader. Packed with the latest e-book capabilities, you'll be able to search for any word, passage or phrase, highlight key sections and take notes that you can print later—all kept together and available on any electronic device.

Audio Edition

Listening and reading are two different experiences, so we created the audiobook to help you *live* the experience. Jerry and Jeff will be right there with you, taking you through everything from your initial search to growing your thriving franchise operation. Jerry will whisper in your ear before your corporate visit, to help you get the most out of franchise training. He'll be there in the car with you as you look for the perfect location for your new business. Jeff will help you stay focused on the business fundamentals to ensure you stay in control of the process every step of the way. With the latest audiobook features, you'll be able to stop the track at any time, type a quick note or even record a voice note.

www.liveit2ownit.com

The L2O website is your portal to the world of franchising. Continuously updated, the site will keep you in the know about the latest developments in the franchise world and point you to the best search and evaluation resources available.

WHO SHOULD READ THIS BOOK?

Whether you are just starting out, investing in an existing franchise or making the move to expand your current operation, this book is for you!

Live It 2 Own It is your personal guide to what really matters in selecting the franchise opportunity that's right for you.

Deciding to invest in or expand an independent business involves much more than finding a hot franchise opportunity, running a few numbers and figuring out what you'll do with all the profits. A franchise operation is a complex and often all-consuming effort that shouldn't be taken lightly.

Live It 2 Own It is designed to help you every step of the way. Use it as your companion, mentor and coach throughout your franchise journey.

HOW TO READ THIS BOOK

Thank you for purchasing *Live It 2 Own It*.

The knowledge in this book, like a franchise business, isn't yours simply because you pay a fee. Handing you the set of keys doesn't make you a business owner. Having employees doesn't make you a business owner. Customers don't make you a business owner (but they are nice to have around). Businesses aren't purchased—they are earned. To earn a franchise business, you must be willing to win, to go all-in from day one. You must be willing to LIVE IT. You must be willing to Live It 2 OWN IT.

No matter your background or experience level, one thing is certain: You don't know what you don't know, and there's not enough time in the day to learn everything you'll need to know without help. That's why L2O is designed to get you the information you need when you need it. Read the book and do the activities from cover-to-cover and you'll have a solid foundation for building a thriving franchise operation. You'll know the questions to ask and where to find the answers.

L2O is your franchise coach—a resource to guide you through the evaluation, selection, operation and growth of your franchise. With hundreds of thousands of franchise opportunities to choose from, no two franchise journeys are exactly alike. We've made every effort to provide you with the information and advice you need to make the major decisions all prospective franchisees face, while avoiding specific brand, industry or technical advice that might not be applicable to you.

After reading this book, you may find that a franchise operation isn't for you—and that's okay. Franchising isn't a good fit for many otherwise talented and energetic businesspeople. If franchising *is* your calling, you'll want to do everything in your power to give yourself the very best chance at success. So, don't just read this book—OWN IT! Make notes, complete every chapter activity and test what you've learned.

This book wasn't written on a whim over a weekend—it's a mission that took years. The insights and advice reflected on these pages are not limited to the personal experience of the authors, but include insights gleaned from hundreds of franchise professionals representing every aspect of franchising. We spoke with some of the most successful franchisors (ZORs), the people that developed franchise opportunities you'll be considering. We interviewed high performing franchisees (ZEEs), consultants and legal professionals. In short, we didn't set out to write a book. We accepted the L2O challenge.

We LIVED IT.

We OWNED IT.

And now we are excited to SHARE IT!

FEATURES

Throughout the book we've included recurring features. The purpose of these features is to help you navigate the content, understand your place in each chapter and explain the work you'll need to accomplish along the way. After your initial reading, these features will help you use the book as a reference tool to find what you are looking for quickly.

AKERS OF ADVICE

The first section in each chapter is titled *Akers of Advice,* followed by a chapter-specific subheading. These sections introduce the central topic and theme of the chapter, in the context of Jerry's experience. In these sections, Jerry shares his experiences and what led him to become one of the nation's leading franchise experts.

THE BIG IDEA

The Big Idea sections focus on the nuts and bolts of the process. Drawing on three decades of global business experience, Jeff will explain the practical and tactical mechanics of the process.

ACTIVITIES

There's nothing passive about pursuing a franchise opportunity. So, we've designed a series of activities for you to accomplish along the way. After you've completed the reading, the activities will help you generate the information and ideas you'll need to share your vision, enlist the help and support of others and build your business plan.

SPOTLIGHT

Spotlight features the personal stories of experienced franchise professionals. From a former NFL pro turned sub sandwich franchisee to a single mom who was fired at 40, started her own franchise system at 54 and today helps run a billion-dollar franchise operation, their unique perspectives both inform and entertain.

READY, SET, PREPARE!

We get it. We've been there. You are ready to get moving. You are ready to fire up your browser and get to work searching for the perfect franchise opportunity. Ready to hit the return button on your keyboard and generate some search results. There's just one small problem, you are not ready. Not yet.

The identification, selection, launch, operation and expansion of a franchise business is a big, complex and time-consuming effort. The process is often confusing and always emotional. The single best way to ensure your success is preparation. The first three chapters of this book focus on what needs to be done before you begin your formal search. You'll learn how and why you need to develop a personal story, identify the people most critical to your success, create a people plan and, most importantly, learn what franchising is and is not.

Table of Contents

FOREWORD:
PETER HOLT, THE JOINT CHIROPRACTIC PRESIDENT & CEO

'm a big believer in the power of common sense. I think that's why I was drawn to the simplicity and logic of the franchising approach. As I learned early on, franchising is not an industry, but an operational model used to rapidly accelerate the development of business concepts. Instead of doing all the work of building, operating and expanding a new business, a franchisor packages a concept and sells operating licenses to people that want to run their own businesses, but don't want to start from scratch.

If everyone does their job, the model is a win-win. The concept developer wins because they are able to grow at a much faster rate. Franchisees win because they can reduce the risks associated with starting a new business.

During my career, I have grown franchise concepts in multiple industries, everything from business and postal communications to frozen yogurt and health services. Now, I'm lucky enough to be part of one of the fastest growing franchises in the business. The Joint Chiropractic has revolution-ized access to chiropractic care, offering affordable membership plans and packages for patients seeking pain relief and ongoing wellness with walk-in convenience. As President and CEO, I've had the privilege of guiding the development of our franchise system since 2016 and watching our network explode, from just eight clinics in 2010 to 639 clinics today, while performing over eight million spinal adjustments in 2020 alone!

Franchising has been such a big part of my life since the very beginning of my career. Frankly, it's difficult to remember a time where I didn't feel like it was made just for me! Reading through the pages of Live It 2 Own It, I was transported back to my early days, back to the excitement and hope that propelled me into my franchising career.

This book paints an accurate and compelling picture of the franchise landscape, illustrating how all parts and pieces relate to one another. The humanness of the franchise experience comes through on every page, which is so critical as franchising is truly the story of real people venturing into the unknown. It's a scary proposition for anyone. You can see it when a new franchisee completes their due diligence and is ready to put it all on the line for their first operating license. For some, it's one of the largest financial decisions they have ever made. They're scared to death, and they should be. Not because franchising is inherently risky but because, after the spreadsheets have been reviewed, after all the discussions and nego- tiations are done, after the check clears and that new franchisee opens their doors for the first time, the success of the business rests firmly on their shoulders.

Thirty-five years have passed since my first exposure to franchising.

It was love at first sight.

Franchising had me at "hello."

Since then, I've spent most of my career in small box retail—units that are one or two thousand square feet, anchored by a big box retailer or supermarket chain; local shops where people stop in to get a haircut, buy a frozen yogurt or send a package. These little spaces can be so many things, and so common that we might not think much about them at all. Yet, if you could look behind the windows and see the human stories behind the businesses, you would see the commitment of family, friends and staff; you'd see the bravery and courage of an entire community of business leaders overcoming fear and self-doubt, all for the chance to *Live It 2 Own It.*

-Peter Holt

THE BRAIN CLIPPER
RESISTANCE IS FUTILE!
YOU WILL CALL JERRY
.....AND LEAVE ME A BIG TIP!
Deidre
SMALL BUSINESS IS
BIG BUSINESS
IN FEEL-O-VISION!

INTRODUCTION:
COMING TOGETHER

Welcome to *Live It 2 Own It*!

This book is the result of a journey that started with a single interview and blossomed into a lifelong collaboration. *Live It 2 Own It* represents our sincere effort to provide you with a comprehensive franchise resource. While the book centers on helping prospective franchisees and existing owners and operators succeed, there is a larger and more important message. It is a message of hope and possibility. It's about a better way to live and grow profitable, people-centered businesses. And it all started when I met a man named Jerry Akers.

I can only imagine the journey that's brought you to these pages. If your experience is like mine, the path that led you to franchising was filled with unexpected twists and turns. My name is Jeff Kaplan and I'll be here alongside Jerry to help you navigate your franchise journey. Like you, my route to franchising was both surprising and unexpected.

I've been working as an author and global business consultant for nearly 30 years. During my career, I've had the privilege of working with many of the greatest organizations on the planet and seeing firsthand how the world's top executives do what they do—global, fast-paced, exciting and always interesting. My daily commutes have taken me past Nelson Mandela's presidential residence in Johannesburg, South Africa, and across the Bosporus Strait on the Martyrs Bridge in Istanbul. I've partied on the top deck of Singapore's iconic Marina Bay Sands Hotel, a complex supported by three 57-story towers fashioned to look like a cruise ship sailing across the sky, and I've rung the bell at the New York Stock Exchange. It never got old.

I'd grown accustomed to riding in the pointy end of the plane, having the flight crew address me by name and, occasionally, getting an invite to tag along on the company jet. I ran with the big dogs and had a seat at the cool kids' table. In my mind, real business was big business; skyscraping, 24-7, globe-spanning operations with toplines that rivaled the gross domestic product of small countries.

This was my world. I knew what worked and what didn't. I knew how to build the machine and make it hum; what to do and what to avoid. I later learned that there's danger in expertise. Danger in mastery. Danger in the unconscious belief that our way is right, true and unchanging—the one best way. It's like reaching into a pile of coins, selecting one and flipping it in the air, sure in the knowledge of how the coin will land. Tails every time. We see only one-sided coins and overlook the possibilities represented by the flip side. Worse, we totally dismiss the mass of opportunities presented by all the other coins in the pile. That was me—before I met Jerry Akers.

I'd worked hard, mastered my craft and was as certain about my beliefs as a one-sided coin. Then I met Jerry. In the space of two years, I discovered the flip side of the coin—a more human and in many ways more successful way of doing business.

APRIL 2016—I saw a little row of signs along the road advertising a sale on haircuts. No appointment necessary, all cuts $9. What more did I need to know? I followed the signs, went in and the greeter told me there was currently no wait. I took a seat; the stylist started her work and the typical chair-chat began. "What do you do for a living?" she asked mid-snip.

"I write business books about the world's best-run companies and the people that lead them. For my new book I've interviewed 1,200 executives in 26 countries," I said, admittedly self-absorbed.

"Wow, that's great. You know, you should interview the owners of our salon. They are a husband-and-wife team. They own a chain of salons. Such amazing people! They'd be perfect for your book. I'll give you their number."

Having the good sense not to vocalize my response, I thought, "Yeah, sure. I'll interview the owners of a small town quick-cuts outlet, you bet. I'll just mix their insights right in there with the wisdom of the world's top business executives. On it!"

Instead, I said. "That would be great. Thank you."

At the register, the stylist handed me her card and showed me she'd written the owner's number on the back. I politely took the card and later trashed it.

I continued working on my book and began to realize something had changed. The people I interviewed were opening up to me in a whole new way. Typically, business interviews are superficial—highlight reels that mask as much as they reveal. Everyone's on their best behavior. Interviewers want to build trust with the person being interviewed and the subjects want to frame their story and accomplishments in the best possible light.

The balance was shifting from the enterprise to the individual. The stories I was now hearing were deeply personal, saturated with fear, uncertainty and doubt. Employees recounted the harms they experienced at the hands of a faceless and everchanging cast of corporate decisionmakers.

Ousted leaders, stripped of title and exiled from the executive suite, struggled to sell themselves to new organizations. Promotions going to unproven outsiders over dedicated managers with long tenures. Individual workers suddenly displaced by the latest round of downsizing. From the boardroom to the breakroom, employed and unemployed, it was becoming clear that our relationship with work was broken.

I called to congratulate one young executive who'd just completed his master's degree. His response was surprising, but consistent with an emerging pattern.

> "Thanks, Jeff. I know I should be more excited, but all it really means is a small raise. Nobody really knows I'm here. I don't have any visibility or any chance to show my capabilities. I've been sitting here in the same cubical for years. My desk chair butts up against a concrete support column. So, if I forget it's there and swivel my chair one way or the other, I'll bang my knee. The problem is I can't say anything. I can't complain or threaten to quit because there's a line of people out there ready to take my job. Seriously, when we hold job fairs, there's literally a line around the block. Sure, I'm thankful that I have work but there must be something more. You are a business guy; do you know anything about franchising?"

It doesn't take much to imagine yourself in the same situation and feel what he was feeling. It might even be the situation you are in right now.

Here are a few of the comments I heard.

"There has to be more than this!"

"I need to find an opportunity that can't be taken away in a heartbeat. Taken away by someone I don't know and who doesn't know me."

"If I ran things, I wouldn't treat people like this."

"I just need a chance to prove myself."

"It's time for me to start my own business. I just don't know how to get started."

"I've ben thinking about starting my own thing. What do you think about franchising?"

Do any of these statements resonate with you?

The more I heard, the more I realized that these folks were giving voice to why, a decade before, I'd exchanged my comfortable corporate job for the uncertain future of starting my own firm. They were describing how I'd felt when I decided to stop making money for other people to build something of my own.

DECEMBER 2016—I relocated 70 miles north of where I'd been living. Soon I found myself in another small town quick-cuts salon. My stylist, Deidre Layfield introduced herself and we started to engage in the same conversation I'd had months ago. I glanced over my shoulder toward the front door and saw the sign; I'd come to the same chain as I had before and our chat ended with the same recommendation, "You should interview the owners of this salon. They are a husband-and-wife team and they'd be great for your book."

This was the second time someone heard what I do and responded by suggesting that I talk to the owners of this chain. Even so, I'm not sure I would have ever followed up if it weren't for what happened next. At the register, Deidre offered me her card just like the other stylist had. On the back of the card was the owners' phone number, just like it was written before. But what happened next was different. When I went to take the card, Deidre held onto it, looked me in the eye and said, "You *really* need to talk to them. They are the kind of people you should be writing about. They do so much for the people who work here. This isn't just a business. You see these women (waving her free hand toward the other stylists)? This is a family. We feel safe here. That's what they've built. This is the kind of company you should be writing about."

This time, instead of trashing the card, I made the call. A few months later, my GPS led me to a suburban strip mall in Cedar Rapids, Iowa. I parked in front of what looked like an unoccupied storefront. Other than a few tables, chairs, a whiteboard and a coffee pot, the unit looked vacant. In the window hung a handwritten sign that read Training Center. Peering through the window for a closer look, I saw a man's head out of a back-office door. Emerging with a warm smile and a wave, the man made his way to the door. I remember thinking, "What have I gotten myself into?"

Jerry opened the door and welcomed me in. After a few pleasantries, the formal interview began. Jerry shared details of his prior life as a corporate executive and recounted the moment he realized the need to strike out on his own. Like Howard Beale, the character played by Peter Finch in the movie Network, Jerry said he was "mad as hell" and he wasn't going to play the corporate game one more day. Jerry and his wife Mickey set out to build the business together. Jerry found the locations, coordinated the buildouts and developed the employee training program. Mickey became the company's Chief Hugs Officer (it's the title printed right on her card) focused on daily operations and employee relations. She starts every employee visit with—you guessed it—a hug.

I've been around for a while, and along the way I've developed a healthy skepticism. Things that look too good to be true, are too good to be true. I knew if I just waited long enough, the other shoe would drop, a crack would form and I'd see Jerry's angle. Minutes stretched to hours. Unlike the data-driven corporate talk-tracks I was accustomed to hearing, Jerry's success stories seldom included performance metrics. Success to Jerry and Mickey, it seemed, genuinely came from the achievements of their employees:

"We were in tears when we heard she was approved for her first home."

"Some of our stylists are just starting out and may not have had the support each of us deserves. They may not know how to balance their checkbook, how to save for a big purchase, or apply for a loan. We'll help do that or whatever they need."

"Our trainings aren't just about learning to do the latest cut, but how to take control over what they earn and how to manage what they earn. We don't push or preach; we're here to listen and look for ways to help."

"A skilled stylist can give a great cut. But a skilled stylist that's working toward a goal, taking charge of their life in ways they'd never imagined and feeling like they are part of a family that cares about them—that stylist is the key to building a great business!"

Jerry's approach was the flip side of the coin. His family-oriented, people-first business model was the antithesis of the big business approach I'd known.

Consider Jerry's description of his annual company party:

"We're a service business, open seven days a week. We have to be. The only time we close all 28 shops is for the Christmas party, and it's not some bowl of punch and homemade cookies thing. It's held at the best hotel in the area and it's a fancy event. For some of the employees this is the first time they've been to a formal event, or it may be the only time they get to dress up the whole year. For us, it's the only time all year that the whole family is together under one roof. On paper it makes no sense for us to hold an event like this, but in terms of its effect on our employees it's the best investment we've ever made."

The interview moved from helping employees to helping other franchisees. I learned that Jerry spends several months on the road each year, flying to markets across the country to help other franchisees succeed.

"There it is," I thought, "There's the hook. He's selling what he knows to create a second revenue stream—that's where the business guy's been hiding!"

I then learned he wasn't offering up his help for cash, in fact he was seldom paid for his time and often covered his own travel expenses just to help someone else.

Long past our scheduled time, we talked, laughed, compared notes and charted ideas on his whiteboard. When I finally convinced him to talk about financial performance, I realized his approach worked for the bottom line, too. He was killing the numbers. The performance of his small-town units consistently ranked among the best in the nation.

I gave up.

I surrendered my skepticism and replaced it with the belief in a better way.

The stylists had been right. I really did need to bring Jerry's insights and approach to a larger audience, just as Deidre advised. Jerry wasn't just telling me how he runs his small business. He was laying out the parameters of a new social contract. He was describing the new rules of work; rules that not only raise the bottom line but raise the quality of life for every member of the organization in the process. He was a small-town boy sharing his family recipe, a recipe for a business model that aligns personal and professional success.

Jerry also held the answer for people who don't just want to work in a people-first organization but want to build one from the ground up. Jerry was presenting a solution for a growing number of people who want a chance to call the shots, to experience what it feels like to build something that can't be taken away on a whim—to make a mark!

So, if you're done with other people deciding your value and controlling your future. If you know, deep down inside that you've waited long enough. If you have the fire, the drive and the guts to put yourself on the line. It's time you ...

Live It 2 Own It!

Boyz' Life

FOR ALL BOYZ

THE ROAD TO COOPERSTOWN!

ONE LITTLE BOY'S BIG DREAM

CHAPTER 1:
WHAT'S YOUR STORY?

W hether you allow us to guide your journey or select another resource—stick with it. If you end up finding the ideal franchise opportunity or find that franchising isn't your thing, you owe it to yourself to be sure you've made the right decision.

You've already decided that the idea of franchising may be right for you, that's likely what brought you to these pages. This book will compare your idea of franchise ownership against the reality of operating a franchise. You'll come to understand the idea of business ownership is very different than the reality of putting the keys in the door and doing what it takes day after day to make your business a success.

We're here to make the process as easy as possible for you. But you aren't off the hook. Making the process easy doesn't mean the process will be easy. It's not.

There are no short cuts, and even if there were we wouldn't advise you to take them. Franchising is a complex puzzle that always seems to have a few missing pieces. This book is the picture on the puzzle box, a guide to what you are trying to piece together. We'll show you how to find the flat-edge pieces, identify the corners, build the border and fill in the middle as your new business takes shape.

In this chapter you will meet Jerry, learn his story and begin to build your own. You'll learn about story selling and the power of personal stories. At the end of the chapter, you'll create the first draft of the story that will serve as the centerpiece of your franchise journey.

AKERS OF ADVICE: JERRY'S STORY

Like many small business owners, I didn't start out that way. I'm just a farm boy from Iowa. My first foray into the business world was at nine-years-old. Growing up on a struggling family farm, my parents often reminded me that money doesn't grow on trees. Financially, it was impossible for my mom and dad to give me some of the extra things that young boys want, but I was like Ralph (Ralphie) Parker, the little boy in *A Christmas Story* that was smitten with a picture he'd seen in a magazine. With the singular focus that only a nine-year-old boy could muster, Ralphie dreamed of getting the Red Ryder Carbine-Action Two-Hundred-Shot Range Model Air Rifle. That was me!

I played baseball and dreamed of a big-league career and what my baseball card would look like. I even practiced the various poses. Action Jerry turning the double play. Home-run Jerry, end of a massive swing, eyes to the sky. Suave Jerry, standing casually leaning on my bat like a walking stick.

The only thing missing, aside from major league talent (simply a minor detail), was a new glove ... and not just any glove. My Ralphie-eyes knew the exactly-most-perfectly-wonderful-absolutely-ideal glove, and it was right there on the pages of the February 1965 edition of Boys' Life. It was so obvious really, to me and anyone who could see what I saw. That glove was the only thing that stood between me and my induction into

Cooperstown, baseball's hall of fame. There was only one problem, like Ralphie, I was only nine and had no money. Zero, bupkis, nada.

Luckily, *Boys' Life* got me.

Boys' Life knew me.

Boys' Life understood my situation and provided the answer.

Big as day, the headline on the next page read: "DO YOU NEED MONEY?"

"Why, yes! Yes, I do," my nine-year-old-self answered.

It couldn't be simpler. *Boys' Life* offered me the audacious sum of $100. More than enough to get my glove and have more money in my pocket than I'd ever dreamed. All I had to do was sell 100 boxes of Gorgeous Greeting cards. All-occasion greeting cards, what could be simpler? And *Boys' Life* told me all I needed to hear.

"Costs nothing to try. Send NO MONEY. We trust you."

I was 100 quick and easy sales away from the glove of my dreams. I didn't need permission. I didn't need to wait for Santa to come through. Besides in those days in our home, Santa was delivering clothes and other necessities and I was looking for the good stuff. I had the answer, and no one could stop me.

I signed up. My kit showed up. I was ready.

Rural Iowa in the mid-1960s wasn't the metropolis people imagine when they think of today's Iowa. I lived right on the border between no place and nowhere. I rode my little bike over many, many, many miles of gravel roads. If you've ever been to Iowa, you may know the area I covered. On one side, there were corn fields (and still are) and on the other side was more corn fields (and still are) and there was often a mile between houses. I had to knock on doors—do anything and everything I could to sell those cards.

I lived in a community of family farmers, money was tight and sales were few and far between. Slowly, I came to the realization that maybe selling 100 boxes wasn't going to happen. Luckily, there was also a point system where I could earn one point for every box I sold, and I only needed 30 points to make it all come together. A lot of hard work on a lot of very hot days paid off. Looking back, I probably made a few pennies an hour but none of that mattered when that box showed up at my door. I used that mitt all the way through high school and into college.

It was much more than a mere baseball glove—it was a symbol of the possible. And it was mine. Well-earned and hard won, I still have that baseball mitt today. My *Boys' Life* glove holds a place of honor in my home because it reminds me of what it takes to achieve a dream—dogged, relentless focus and a never-ever-say-die attitude.

The Chicago Cubs never came calling, and I missed my induction into the Hall of Fame, but I've never regretted that experience and what it taught me. It made me a better businessperson and a better father. Making the connection between a big hairy dream and the wondrous satisfaction of seeing that dream come true was an experience I still draw on today and you can too.

No matter what we do or what we are trying to achieve, we're always earning points. Whether you are working with a bank to borrow the money you need, expanding your franchise or you're peddling greeting cards to earn your dream mitt, the points we earn mark the path toward the ultimate business goal.

Dollar or dinar, rand or ruble, peso or pound; money isn't the only way to keep score and it's not the real destination. Every day what we choose to do and, just as importantly, what we choose not to do, add and subtract from our point total and decide what we get and what we can't have. It's all about choice.

Choice is the ultimate goal of the successful businessperson.

Want to start-up a new business? No problem.

Want to expand your current business? No worries.

Want to leave your kids with a way to earn a living for the rest of their lives? The choice is yours.

How do businesspeople earn points? We out produce, out learn and outsmart our competition. If we do that, the money will follow. Our goal is to create the single best resource for developing, launching, operating and expanding your franchise business. Beyond the pitch, promise and prospectus; there's so much more to making the cut in the world of franchise ownership. So, jump on your bike and get ready to pedal. The road is long and it may get hot. There will be times your dream mitt seems out of reach, but we'll be there with you, door after door.

Door #1.

What's your story?

Everything you do, every step of the way, your story will help others get to know you better, understand what you are trying to accomplish and why it's so important to you.

THE BIG IDEA: STORY SELLING

About ten years ago, Jeff had the opportunity to participate in the development of what would become legendary film producer Peter Guber's #1 New York Times bestselling book *Tell to Win*. In the early stages of the project, Peter shared how he'd come to produce films like *Batman, The Color Purple, Gorillas in the Mist, Midnight Express* and *Rain Man*. Peter credited the power of stories as the central driver of his success, taking him from Columbia Pictures to the chairmanship of Sony Pictures, and ultimately, to the founding of Mandalay Entertainment Group.

Mastering the facts and making the case for commercial viability are table stakes. What it takes to win and stay winning comes from a businessperson's ability to tell human stories that underpin business activity. Story selling is at the heart of everything we do.

Are you single? You're a storyseller!

Have an idea for a local event? You're a story seller!

Wanna build your dream business and win the help and support of others to make it a reality? You are a story seller!

Personal or professional, the most important story you'll ever tell is the story of YOU. From family and friends to customers and colleagues, you need to be prepared to tell your story again and again.

- What should your story include?
- Where did it all start?
- How did you get from where you were to where you are today?
- Why do you want to own your own business?
- What is your vision for your business?
- What good will your business accomplish aside from generating wealth?

Your story should touch on your prior experience and highlight both your successes and your failures. If the truth is that you're driven by a chip on your shoulder, that you have something to prove, don't be shy—you're in good company. Above all, be honest. You'll tell this story again and again. People sense insincerity. They know when something feels false. Be yourself—warts and all.

Too often we hide who we are for fear of being judged. Muster the confidence to share the real you, and you'll likely be surprised at the responses you receive. Of course, we're not suggesting you mention your second cousin's career as an underworld kingpin or detail your youthful indiscretions, but to tell your story, you have to *tell your story*.

As a business owner, people want to know the person they'll be investing in, working for and buying from. Friends and family will want to understand your motivation and why their support is so critical to your success. You'll be asked to tell your story when you apply for a loan and work with real estate people. Potential employees will be interested in their new boss.

You're about to transform your personal vision into a living, breathing business. One thing is for sure—you won't get there alone. If you want others to believe in your vision, they must first believe in you.

So, when you're asked, "What's your story?" ...

Will you be clear, confident and prepared? Or will you wing it?

ACTIVITY: MY STORY

Create a first draft of your story. Don't worry, no one will read it until you are ready to share it. Grammar and spelling don't count, and there's only one wrong answer—not completing the exercise. Like many things in life, you'll never have a better opportunity to set the foundation for your new business than right now, right at the start. Preparation is what separates wannabees from serious players.

Remember this is just a draft, a place to start, something to keep in mind as you progress. As you broaden your understanding of franchise operations, you'll likely reconsider your draft and make changes—that's the whole idea.

Q: What's the right length for my story?
A: Think three to five minutes.

You should be able to share your story in no more than five minutes.

Your story should be three to five paragraphs (or 300-500 words) in length.

Once you've completed your story, take a moment and read it aloud. Sound good? Sound like you? Is it honest? Does it clearly show how you got here and why? If not, that's okay. Return to your draft at the end of each chapter and ask yourself if what you've learned calls for a revision. By the time you've completed the book, you'll have a story you can be proud to tell again and again.

SPOTLIGHT: THE CREATOR, ELLEN LATHAM

A familiar circumstance. An unexpected response.

As a lifelong exercise enthusiast, Ellen Latham worked her way up the ladder to become manager of a high-end fitness spa in Miami Beach. She had her dream job. Her professional life was great.

Until it wasn't.

Everything changed when she learned that the gym she managed had been sold and that the new owners wouldn't be requiring her services. A familiar circumstance for too many otherwise top tier workers who pay the price for shortsighted corporate decision making.

With a wave of a bureaucratic wand, Ellen went from upwardly mobile executive to out-of-work-40-something-single-mom with few choices. She could take her lumps and start over again with another organization or do something unexpected. With Ellen's go-big-or-go-home personality it wasn't surprising that she chose the latter. *Unexpectedly responding* to her job loss by developing an entirely new franchise concept—Orangetheory Fitness Studio.

When faced with a career crossroad, Latham made a choice familiar to franchise professionals. She chose to invest in her own abilities and go it alone. "I decided I would work for myself and become an entrepreneur." Proof that even the biggest ideas often have humble beginnings, Ellen started out giving private Pilates sessions in a spare bedroom and running a spin program she created at a local gym. Her following steadily grew and soon, with the help and support of her loyal customers and a modest loan, Latham opened her own studio.

"This is where it's so important, especially in business, to listen your customer. My customers were telling me that they loved how I formatted group fitness for spinning and Pilates, but they weren't getting the fat burning and metabolic work that they really desired." Ellen listened and drawing from her bachelor's and master's degrees in exercise science, designed what she called The Ultimate Workout. The response was incredible.

Her clientele was enthusiastic and encouraged her to think bigger. One client, whose husband was a franchise executive told her a fitness studio this popular, that generated the results Ellen's studio was getting, should be on every corner. Ellen listened and became an overnight success in just twenty-five short years. Fourteen years to develop the workout system and 11 years to build the franchise model. Today, Orangetheory Fitness has become a billion-dollar fitness franchise system with 1,400 studio locations in 22 countries that serve 800,000 members.

The secret behind her success? Ellen says the three P's guide her as a businesswoman: *people, processes* and *programs*. Based on all that she's learned, she knows, "if a franchisor gets these three right, things fall into place. My partners and I hired the right *people* to create the right *processes*, like how franchisees should find studio space, conduct pre-sales activities and ultimately open the doors with the most effective *programs* available."

Latham still applies the three P's today. "We look for franchisees who have a passion for physical fitness. We encourage them to hire managers and staff with a similar mindset to attract members who will realize there's something special about the Orangetheory program—from the unique workout to the supportive atmosphere."

To ensure you select the franchise that's right for you, Ellen suggests selecting a franchise system that is going to be there for you when you need them. "Don't take anyone's word for it. Investigate for yourself. Explore the relationships between the ZOR and ZEEs that operate in the system. If the ZOR has invested in great people, developed great processes and created programs to effectively support franchisee efforts, then you can feel a little more confident in making your decision."

Ellen's best advice for career success? Do what you love! The rest will follow. "Sure, I loved building a very successful brand, but I didn't get into the fitness business 45 years ago to create the next big fitness franchise. My goal has always been to create phenomenal fitness in human bodies—that's the most exciting to me because that's exactly what we're doing. I wouldn't change anything."

CHAPTER 2:
TEMPO EFFECT

S uccess is not a solo activity. Wherever and whatever you hope to achieve, *you cannot get there alone.* Therefore, becoming success-ful requires learning how to foster the resources and develop the relationships you'll need to become a successful franchise operator. You'll discover the power of the TEMPO Effect, a central component of Jeff's leadership and sales training program delivered in 26 countries around the world. TEMPO-setting executives consistently *outlearn, outperform* and *out-earn* the competition—and now you can too! The TEMPO effect is what happens when great businesspeople master the art of leveraging and aligning other people's *Time, Expertise, Money, People* and *Opportunities* to create mutual support for mutual success. You'll learn how to apply the TEMPO Effect to rapidly accelerate the development of your franchise operation.

AKERS OF ADVICE: ZORS, ZEES AND ZUPER HEROES!

In the franchise business, franchisors (the organizations that develop the brands and operating systems) are referred to as ZORs. The enterprising businesspeople that purchase franchise licenses are called franchisees or ZEEs for short. I've always liked those nicknames because they remind me of comic book characters. Go ZORs! Go ZEEs! ZUPER heroes unite!

When you think about it, the comparison isn't much of a stretch because creating franchise systems and building franchise businesses are superhuman feats. I grew up on superhero comic books. The stories of incredible heroes brought to life courtesy of DC and Marvel. I wasn't hayseed enough to believe that they were real. In fact, it was the suspension of disbelief that made it even more exciting. For Superman, the impossible was commonplace; doing the right thing wasn't making a hard decision from many choices—it was gloriously simple, the right honorable way, and the only choice he ever made.

Those colorful pages challenged my young mind to imagine what could be; to believe that somewhere out there, beyond what I could see, beyond what I'd ever known, the most magnificent adventures were waiting to unfold. My real eyes saw a single-featured horizon, 360°of cornfield meeting sky. Batman, Spiderman, the Flash took me beyond what my eyes said was there.

Page by heart-thumping page, my heroes faced unbelievable challenges and almost always won (if not this episode, then certainly the next or the one after). Superhero tales didn't just entertain, they transported. Between those pages I wasn't sitting cross-legged with my back against the barn in the middle of an Iowa cornfield. I was out there where the action was, fighting the good fight and always making the right choice—doing the right thing for truth, justice and the American way.

You might not share my nostalgic love of comics. For you it might be books, a TV series, movie or the words of your amazing Grandma, the advice of a teacher who took the time to care. The possibilities are infinite, but one thing is for sure: If you are reading this book, you've come to a point in your life that you're seriously considering franchise ownership, and someone, somewhere along the line, helped you believe you had the power to make your dreams a reality.

Comic books were my gateway drug. It didn't take me long to graduate to the hard stuff, comic books without the comic. I remain a voracious reader today. I read real books—the hardbound tree-killing tomes. My books don't light up and can't be stored in the cloud. I read books that take up space, weigh-down my suitcase, fill up my bookshelves and find their way into every nook and cranny of my life and make moving worse than it already is. I've read and reread all the business classics. Along the way, I've developed deep one-way relationships with Zig Ziglar, Stephen Covey and all the greats. I not only bought the business classics but bought into what they were selling. I learned how to think to grow rich and how to practice each of *the seven habits*, but I've always rejected the notion of self-made man.

In 1832, Senator Henry Clay coined the phrase to describe the power of personal determination, that success lay within us, not out there. There's no denying that motivation is a critical success factor, but the idea of a self-made man simply doesn't jive with my experience. I've known lots of very successful men and women—my wife and daughters among them. Yet I have never, not once, seen an example of someone achieving real success alone. It simply doesn't happen. A member of your family comes through with a small loan; a friend's good word results in a critical order; a mentor's advice helps avoid catastrophe.

Success.

Every part.

Every piece.

Every step.

Everything we have and everything we don't have.

All result from our interactions with others.

Sure, sometimes we get bad advice. We may witness examples of what not-to-do and pray to ourselves, "Please, please, don't ever let me end up like that." It's all valuable information you can use to help guide your franchise journey.

Oliver Napoleon Hill extolled us to *Think and Grow Rich*. Implicit in his advice is that somewhere inside us, we believe in ourselves. We believe that we can be more, accomplish more and that we have the strength to find the truth and do what's right. Most folks find comfort and safety in the familiar, but people like us are compelled to venture out. Some wait at the river's edge and others toe-test the water. Entrepreneurs do neither. We are the all-or-nothing, take a running-start and dive right-in crowd. We are the ones who must know:

Do I have the right stuff?

I'm in the water waving you in; it's cool and crisp in here, and—perfect for a swim.

I'm calling to you, "No risk, no reward!"

But I'm also a grown-up and the kind of friend that cares enough to ask, "Can you swim?"

If you take the plunge, I'll guide you along the way. I'll help you avoid the big rock that's hidden under the surface of the water. I'll be the first one to wave the caution flag and remind you that "too much risk, too little thought and you'll get crushed like a bug."

Running your own business is a superhero-sized adventure without a net. There are very real dangers ahead—things you can't always see and there's no guarantee you'll make the right choice or do the right thing in this episode, or ever! That's why Jeff and I are here. We've tested the waters, mapped the hazards and made almost every mistake possible—so you don't have to.

I've never met my business heroes. Zig, Napoleon and the other greats don't know me, but I know them. Like my superhero friends, they told the tales of struggle, adversity and daring. Their words transported me out there, put me in the action, showed me how to fight the good fight, make the right choice and do the right thing for truth, justice and the bottom line.

My arms are waving to get your attention.

I'm calling you from the water.

"You can't get there alone. It's time to build the foundation for your future success."

Go ZORs! Go ZEEs! ZUPER heroes, unite!

THE BIG IDEA: THE TEMPO EFFECT

Building a business is a mental game that doesn't come with instructions— for good reason. Like a snowflake, no two businesses or operating units are exactly alike. Each has a unique personality, culture and challenges. As *emotional* as it is *logical*, franchise ownership requires self-motivation, an analytic eye and as much help and support as you can muster. From dealing with the unknown, to securing the resources you'll need, one thing is for sure—you can NOT get there alone.

Over the last three decades I've worked with thousands of successful pro-fessionals—people whose achievements are undeniable by virtually any measure: money, operational scale, relationships, physical fitness—you name it. I've met over-performers from every background and circum-stance but I've *never, not once*, met a single successful businessperson who claims to have made it singlehandedly. Without exception, the stories of those at the top include someone giving them a big break, a mentor who took interest, advice that changed everything, a critical introduction at just the right time—and these business giants have expressed their willingness to help others succeed.

You may feel you already know how to get the most out of your dealings with others—but really, how disciplined is your approach? Becoming more purposeful about your interactions with others, finding ways to align what you need with what they want to create more value from every relation-ship is the difference between competence and mastery.

The TEMPO Effect is what happens when you get more out of every action, more out of every dollar, more out of every relationship. The TEMPO Effect is what happens when you position yourself to accelerate the develop-ment of your business, increase the quality of the decisions you make and secure the financial and human resources you'll need to make it all work. The TEMPO Effect is the power to predictably improve outcomes through the disciplined practice of the TEMPO Mindsets.

Stanford University psychologist Carol Dweck coined the term *mindset* to explain why intelligence and skill aren't enough to ensure success. Mindsets reflect how our self-perception affects our ability to capitalize on opportunities and overcome challenges. Those who believe their skills and abilities are fixed, unnecessarily reduce the likelihood of overcoming obstacles and challenges.

The TEMPO Mindsets are your personal inventory list—an easily accessible reminder of how to get the information and resources you don't have, can't afford or may not even know you need. If you take the TEMPO Mindsets into every meeting, every discussion, every passing hello, you'll be prepared to supercharge your use of Time, Expertise, Money, People and Opportunities to help you and the people you work with do more, learn faster, get greater value from every dollar, build higher-value relationships and identify opportunities others miss.

Understanding the TEMPO Effect and making each of the five mindsets part of everything you do is the best way to ensure that you have what you need to get your business up and running and keep your business healthy and profitable long into the future.

TIME

As an independent business owner, you'll need to manage your time effectively. Business owners set the pace and call the shots. Procrastination is a luxury you can no longer afford. You must take issues head on because you can no longer put off until tomorrow what must be done today—you must adopt the TIME mindset.

The TIME mindset views *time* as a high-value resource which must be used *effectively* to get the most out of every minute of every day, and *efficiently* by focusing on what's really important.

Effective time management focuses on production—*getting things done.*

Efficient time management focuses on prioritization—*getting the right things done.*

The franchise journey we've detailed for you in this book includes a series of specific tasks, some which must be done in sequential order, some which must be accomplished in parallel with other tasks. Some are tasks you can't wait to do; some you should put out of your mind completely in the early stages of your journey and some need to be done without delay.

There are only so many hours in a day—we can't wish, hope, dream or manufacture more. While we can work to become more productive, to stay laser-focused on what's most important, the sheer volume of what needs to be done to effectively run your business simply can't be accomplished by you alone. The only way to increase the time that's available to you is to leverage the time of others. When you think about it, that's exactly what you'll be doing with the employees of your new business. As the employer, you'll be leveraging your employees' time to do what needs to be done to make your business run. In exchange, you'll compensate your employees for the time they focus on your goals.

Your task, like many of the tasks you'll undertake as a business owner, will be to accomplish more than is physically possible for any one person to accomplish. If you are like most business owners, you are likely inclined to do it yourself. You may believe no one can do it as well as you because no one cares as much as you. If I'm right, at some point in your life, someone suggested you might have *control issues*. Someone may have even referred to you as a *control freak* a time or two.

It's time to shed the old you and realize that the size of a business cor-relates with the size of the workforce. The bigger the business, the more people are necessary to get the job done. If you can't let go, can't muster the trust to allow others to do what needs to be done, you'll never grow beyond what you personally can do. Doing it all on your own is not only a bad decision, but it also unnecessarily constrains the growth and prof-itability of your business. Choosing to do it all yourself also creates the conditions for burnout, stress-related health issues and the breakdown of personal relationships.

Don't do it.

Once you've selected the franchise opportunity that's right for you, things will start moving very quickly. One of the first things you'll need to do is develop a business plan. It is rare for a new business owner to possess a firm grasp on every aspect of the business. You may be an expert in sales and marketing, while having little experience in financial planning and human resource management. Even if you are the exception, having func-tional expertise is not the same thing as having the time to organize your knowledge into a coherent plan. Consider breaking down your business plan into its constituent parts: executive summary, company description, products and services, market analysis, strategy and implementation, orga-nizational management and financial projections.

That's a big job.

For those with the TIME mindset, a *big job* isn't a *big problem*. Big tasks are a series of smaller manageable tasks, which can be done quickly and in parallel by leveraging the time of other people. The TIME mindset means taking little for granted, challenging assumptions and asking for help. While your competition feels the heat struggling to find the time to do everything that needs doing, you'll focus on shared objectives and finding ways to get what you want while helping others do the same.

While some business owners listen with a transactional ear, those with the TIME mindset openly share their goals and challenge vendors to discover ways to cooperatively achieve goals. Potential vendors and employees, other business owners, civic and community leaders, educators, friends and family, everyone you know or come into contact with holds the potential to expand what you can do with your most precious resource—TIME.

Learning to leverage what you do to generate value for others is the surest way to claim a disproportionate share of other people's time to help you succeed. Consider how salespeople spend their time. A salesperson doesn't sell to everyone he or she speaks with. For most salespeople it's a numbers game, they speak to many people to complete one or a few transactions. Repeating the same pitch repeatedly, they naturally focus on controlling the conversation, providing readymade answers to buyer objections. Salespeople rarely get the opportunity to flex their business muscles, to discover new ways to apply their product and service knowledge to solve your business problems. Engaging a salesperson to do some of your legwork may mean they have less time to spend with other prospects, but chances are they'll learn something in the process, making him or her a better salesperson. Everyone wins. Besides, if a salesperson can't or won't help you, you've saved yourself from squandering another TEMPO resource MONEY, which we'll get to shortly.

Asking an advertising salesperson to create a report that details how other businesses like yours have successfully and unsuccessfully used his or her product or service in the past is a fair question. Report in hand, you'll not only have a better understanding of what works and what doesn't, you'll also have a list of other business owners you can call—people who can share what they learned from the time they invested to learn it. Provided you are willing to do the same when your phone rings, you'll create a virtuous cycle, expand your network, make better decisions and get things done faster.

How can you use the TIME mindset to develop your franchise business plan?

Do you have time to create a detailed summary of your business concept along with a multi-year profit and loss projection?

How might you extend your time by leveraging the time of others to accomplish these tasks and a host of others we have yet to cover?

As you think through your answers to these questions, you'll begin to see the inextricable connection between leveraging time and experience. While these concepts do overlap, leveraging the expertise of others is a unique and indispensable tool.

EXPERTISE

Chances are you'll hear someone suggest that a franchise is a business in-a-box. Don't be fooled. No matter how structured a franchise system may be, there's a whole universe out there called *execution* that requires a MUCH BIGGER box than the one your franchise system came in.

Regardless of your background, what you did before, where you came from, what school you attended or didn't attend; running an independent business will require new skills and specialized knowledge you've never developed. The fact is, many small business owners have not mastered financial nuance, don't understand implications of a triple-net lease, aren't up to speed on the latest employment regulations or any number of other areas of specialized knowledge. However, the fact that you lack expertise or are unaware of certain regulations and requirements doesn't change your responsibility to get the expertise you lack and abide by legal and regulatory rules.

After you've become an established franchise operator, state and local regulations will change, as will employment and tax law. Single unit operators looking to expand will need a whole new set of capabilities to run a multi-unit operation. Moving from a multi-unit business to take the helm of an entire district, region or multi-state operation (terminology among franchise systems), raises a fresh new set of challenges because franchise businesses, large and small, have an insatiable hunger for specialized expertise.

Unless you come to your new business with an accounting or finance background, it's likely you'll need the support of a good accountant. When interviewing potential accounting firms, ask the candidates to tell you how they've helped other small businesses overcome their most daunting problems. In this case, you may not even know what problems you'll face. Tapping into the knowledge and expertise of potential vendors is one of the best ways to build your own.

The best way to start building your business is to start building the relationships that will sustain it. We're not suggesting you offer vendors a piece of your new business, but we do suggest you approach potential vendors as if they are going to become a part of your business. Accountants know a great deal more than credits, debits and tax strategy. They probably work with many businesses like yours and have learned a great deal in the process—take advantage of this fact. Remember, *taking advantage of* a vendor's full value is not the same thing as taking advantage of that vendor.

The same holds true for builders, bankers and banner makers—whatever they do, *that's what they do, all day, every day*. You'd be doing yourself and your business a disservice not to fully leverage what they do to help develop your own expertise.

Pushing hard to gain new insights and know-how is also a great way to ensure that you choose the right vendors for your business. Lots of accountants can do your books. Some can help you minimize your tax exposure. A few may even connect you with lenders and investors that can help you secure the capital you need. But the vendor that's right for you is the one willing to invest his or her expertise to help you succeed.

MONEY

Money isn't just an issue for small businesspeople. For many it is THE defining issue of business success. Like a movie where an aging detective is killed only one week before his retirement, too many businesses walk a cash tightrope, perilously balancing financial demands against the threat of certain doom. Unless you have great credit, have a home or other personal property you can use for collateral or have a nest egg you are willing to put on the line, chances are you'll need to approach a number of bankers, business investors and even family and friends to secure the money you need to make your business go. No matter the source, there's a cost. Money costs money!

The need for start-up capital and the cost of that capital are concepts you may or may not fully understand. You may have credit card balances, car payments, a mortgage or other debt. You may intuitively understand that a 6% interest rate is less expensive than a 7% interest rate. You may even appreciate the fact that the 6% offer is based on compound interest and the 7% offer is simple interest, going with the higher interest rate may be less expensive and it only gets more complicated from there.

Start-up capital is only one small part of the constant cash diet you'll need to feed your business. Practitioners of the MONEY mindset think about money differently—they seek to get a disproportionate amount of value out of every dollar. Negotiating a lower interest rate, or more favorable terms and even finding ways to get your vendors to put some skin in the game are great ways to make your money work harder, but the MONEY mindset challenges you to dig deeper into the value equation.

Here's an example. You may be thinking about purchasing a radio or television advertising schedule and, while it's a significant investment for you, your investment may not move the needle for the station you are buying from. However, media outlets rarely sell every single spot, every single day. The media industry, being a savvy user of the MONEY mindset, pools unused inventory and awards unpurchased spots to paid advertisers as added value. This pool is often referred to as ROS or run-of-station inventory, spots that run where and when availability exists. To make advertising accessible to smaller business, some media outlets may sell ROS packages that don't guarantee when or where your advertisement will run, only that it will run a certain number of times and be seen by a certain number of people. Like a professional sports draft, your ROS position (first pick or tenth) and whether you have one pick or many, carries real value in terms of advertising effectiveness.

Since advertisers want to sell more advertising, the bigger the buy or the more frequent the purchase, the more attention and benefits the advertiser receives. The smaller the schedule, the fewer the freebies. As a small business owner, your investment alone likely means you can't play with the big dogs, but franchisees with the MONEY mindset are never alone, they don't accept the value equation as is—they change the game by rethinking the small business advertising dilemma.

Franchises that operate in multi-unit commercial properties face an advertising challenge similar to that faced by hotels, resorts and attractions. To fill rooms and sell tickets, travel-based business needs to reach out to customers in many markets, states and even countries. The cost to cast such a wide advertising net makes effective advertising an impossibility. Somewhere along the line, a MONEY mindset-savvy travel marketeer came up with the idea of destination marketing. Entire communities of travel-related business began to pool resources and focus their marketing efforts getting customers interested in coming to the destination in which the businesses operate. A single Las Vegas hotel wouldn't have the resources to advertise nationally, but a group consisting of all the hotels and attractions in Las Vegas could pool their resources to fund a national campaign to attract visitors to the area. Once a customer commits to taking a Vegas vacation, each of the participants would then compete for their share of the spend.

Let's say you have a retail business that operates in a strip mall, a common franchise format. The purpose of your advertising is to drive foot traffic—to get people in your business. Isn't that the same goal as your neighbors' businesses? Using the MONEY mindset, couldn't you use the destination approach? In fact, the solution may work even better for you, because most strip malls don't lease to directly competing tenants. Making your strip mall a destination, where customers can get a quick haircut, grab a sandwich and shop for a new cell phone. This approach is not only convenient for your customers, but the shared advertising expense could move your ROI (return on investment) calculation from no–go to let's go!

The franchise you are considering may not be a retail outlet or lend itself to broadcast media, but the point holds, no matter what you do, the MONEY mindset extends the limits of your resources by changing the rules of the game. People-first thinking and the discovery of a common cause will help you extend the value of every dollar.

See Chapter 8: Marketing, Promotion & You for a detailed discussion of franchise marketing strategy.

PEOPLE

Running an independent business is a rollercoaster ride sure to offer highs and lows. Whether you're up or down, you'll feel like you never have all the resources you need. That's where the PEOPLE mindset comes into play. The PEOPLE mindset is the process of discovering how to align your people with other people's people to create a mutual benefit.

Extending the advertising example from the last section. Let's say you decide to extend the value of your destination marketing approach into your discount strategy. Based on information provided by your ZOR, you know that coupons have been a highly effective tool in drawing new customers for other franchisees in your system. Applying the destination marketing approach, instead of investing in a single flyer containing a coupon or two and focusing entirely on your business, you create a sheet of coupons featuring all the stores in your strip mall. The cost of the flyer would be a fraction of creating one on your own and you'd extend the reach of your distribution by leveraging the resources of the other businesses you've partnered with. The savings might allow you to produce more flyers,

OR you could reinvest your savings by offering a more meaningful discount or other valuable offer.

If your mall-mates go along, you now have a valuable set of coupons. With your PEOPLE mindset thinking cap firmly in place, you ask yourself, who else could benefit from the value you've created? You brainstorm a list of possibilities and one jumps to the top. You decide to transform your coupon flyer into a coupon book—the cost of printing the book in partnership with your mall-mates is still less than a flyer you'd print and distribute on your own. And now that it's a high-value coupon book, you can approach a local charity, club or youth sports team with the idea of selling the book as a fundraiser. You've effectively extended the investment in a single flyer into a coupon book with higher perceived value. You've helped a local charity raise funds and best of all the people that buy the book from the charity may be more likely to redeem a coupon! You've leveraged other people's people (the folks at the charity, club or team) to promote your coupon book and talk about your business.

We're not trying to get ahead of ourselves in talking about the mechanics of marketing your business—we have an entire chapter (Chapter 8) that is packed with proven marketing techniques. The point is that the PEOPLE mindset shouldn't be an afterthought—start with the Mindsets in everything you do. While we've used an advertising example to illustrate the concept, we could just as easily apply the same principles to every part of the business development process.

OPPORTUNITIES

The key to the OPPORTUNITY mindset is uncovering opportunities that other people don't see. Let's say you've decided to sponsor a local minor league baseball team. The deal gives you signage in a stadium, a promotional or themed night focused on your business and tickets to all the home games. You make a great sign, run some awesome promotions and you and your family use the tickets that came along with the sponsorship whenever you can. A reasonable approach for most, but those with the OPPORTUNITY mindset are screaming for more, asking themselves how to leverage the opportunity for more value.

Wouldn't it be great to get pictures of the star player making a great play right in front of your sign? A diving catch, with two outs in the ninth, to win the championship would be great but you'll take what you can get. The team is likely to have a photographer on-site or the local media outlets may have freelancers who work the games but might be willing to take a few shots for you. Even if that isn't in the cards, there are likely several aspiring photographers at the local university or community college, or maybe someone you know is aspiring to be the next Ansel Adams and would jump at the opportunity. Or what if, lucky you, one of the other businesses in your strip mall is a photo shop? That simple sign, the one that the typical business owner puts up and walks away from, can become an opportunity for you to assemble high-value advertising and promotional assets (the amazing-catch-in-front-of-your-sign), while helping an aspiring creative talent develop their portfolio, build their reputation and say to others, "Did you see the picture of that great catch? I took that!" Your MONEY mindset is satisfied because you generated great value for little to no additional cost. In addition, you've now added the photographer (EXPERTISE mindset) to your extended business family and someone invested in the success of your business (PEOPLE mindset).

You get the idea. But let's play this out.

The night of your promotion you arrange for the charity selling your coupons to set-up a few tables during the event to boost their fundraising efforts. At the game you enter the names and contact information of every person that purchases a coupon book into a raffle, and you award the winner a set of the tickets you and your family hadn't been using and collect the raffle entries for your customer prospect database (which you share with your mall-mates).

Now that you've tasted success, you start to see opportunity everywhere. Your OPPORTUNITY mindset won't let a single one of those tickets you're entitled to go unused, so you use the tickets like currency to engage a wider range of people. Top performing employees, vendors, neighboring businesses—all the people that are becoming the support network for your business are invited as your guests. What do you ask in return? Nothing. Well, one small favor. You ask that your guests simply take a selfie of themselves at the game with the scoreboard in the background (guaranteeing your sign will be in the picture) and post the picture on their social media, which you can repost on your Instagram, Twitter and Facebook pages. People are now advertising your brand, providing a personal endorsement and demonstrating that your business is an active and trustworthy member of the local community.

Everyone benefits. You and your business will be seen as a value generator and everyone you worked with this time will be ready to consider your next great idea. Don't get too hung up on the specifics of the examples. You may choose to run a business-to-business franchise that's run out of an industrial center. You might run a home-based business. You might not feel the example is practical or right for your style, that's okay! The point is this:

No matter the structure of your business or the style of your approach, your business will benefit from every resource it can get.

The TEMPO Effect won't make your task list disappear, make you an expert in all things franchise, eliminate your need for cash, produce more human resources than you need or create unlimited opportunity for you and your business, but a disciplined and purposeful application of the TEMPO mindsets will dramatically increase your chances of building a sustainable franchise operation. It may make the process a little more fun, too.

That's why we chose to present this material up front, before we even start talking about the mechanics of selecting, funding, operating and growing your franchise business. In fact, your choice to explore franchise ownership suggests that you may have a predisposition to leverage the TEMPO Effect.

ACTIVITY: DO YOU HAVE A PEOPLE PLAN?

Part of the appeal of franchise ownership is that much of the legwork has been done for you. The name, logo, product, pricing and even hours of operation are often part of the value you receive from your investment. In fact, your decision to become a franchisee is based largely on the concept of leveraging other people's time and expertise. When you purchase a franchise, you are leveraging the time and expertise it took to create the franchise model. You are leveraging the money the ZOR invested in developing and testing the model. The investment is only valuable because of the people who worked to create the opportunity you are now considering. It's important to remember this fact as you start to apply the TEMPO mindsets in your franchise journey.

Over the past 25-years, Jeff has shared the TEMPO mindsets with business-people across the globe. Nearly a quarter-million people have heard the message and made the TEMPO mindsets part of their business tool kit.

Q: When should I start applying the TEMPO mindsets?

A: If you haven't already started thinking about the resources you might
need to build your business, do it now. The activity that follows is
your first step.

Q: How do I organize my TEMPO approach?

A: Even if you don't know the type of franchise you're interested in, some
TEMPO resources are universal. No matter the business, you'll need
help with money (access and management), you'll need legal advice and
human resource know-how. You'll be giving yourself a big leg-up if you
start to identify and organize your resources now and adjust as you go.
The way to organize your TEMPO approach is by creating, what we call, a
PEOPLE PLAN.

Using an electronic spreadsheet or a hand-drawn table, create five columns across the top and label the first column *Time*, the second *Expertise*,
the third *Money*, the fourth *People* and the last column *Opportunity*. Along
the side, label the rows, *Finance, Operations, Human Resources, Marketing*
and *Legal*. You'll likely want to add additional rows as you uncover other
areas of specific importance to your business, but for right now start with
a simple 5 × 5. The resulting table will contain 25 boxes (the intersection of
five rows and five columns). Now take a few minutes and think about the
people you already know or need to meet (a description like lawyer is fine,
if you don't have a business attorney in mind) that might fill each of the
intersecting boxes. It's likely you won't be able to fill your 5 × 5 right now or
even in the next few months, but like all good prep work you've already set
up the tool that will help you build your TEMPO team. And to think, just a
few minutes ago, you might have felt alone in your franchise journey!

SPOTLIGHT: THE PRODIGY JENNIFER KUSHELL

At fifteen, Jennifer Kushell was feeling the pressure. In her mind, it was time to get her act together. Having grown up in a family steeped in franchise history, she's always been interested in running her own business, but the source of her anxiety came from learning that Fred DeLuca, the founder of Subway restaurants had started his company when he was just 17. To Jennifer the math was clear, and the pressure was on. She had only two years, just 24 months, to start building a concept that could impact the world. Fred had shown it was possible, but was she up to the task?

Growing up, Jennifer's father Edward Kushell served as Chairman of the International Franchise Association. Edward tried to include his family in his work by bringing them to conferences and events. The experience exposed Jennifer to every facet of the franchising business and gave her a front row seat to observe industry leaders in action. One of those leaders happened to be Fred DeLuca. Not surprisingly, the two hit it off and became lifelong friends.

While Jennifer didn't make her self-imposed deadline of creating a new global company by age 17, her sharp intellect and businessperson's instincts helped her identify a gap in existing education and support programs with respect to young people. She didn't see many people her age at events; she wasn't aware of any programs to help educate and attract young people to the franchising business, a model heavily dependent on young talent.

Jennifer eventually applied what she learned to help educate and support young people interested in a franchising career. She developed and launched youth-oriented campaigns with brands like Subway, the

International Franchise Association and other big companies like Visa, Ernst & Young and Bloomberg. Today, in partnership with JA Worldwide (www.JAWorldwide.org/EYP), Jennifer is helping millions of students around the world to learn about employment, entrepreneurship and franchising, and to cultivate the leadership skills necessary to take control and ownership of their lives and futures. "I had seen franchising and licensing as business models that were able to scale programs and resources. I thought, why can't we apply a lot of those models to education?"

Kushell's insight proved prescient, "One in five young people begin their career with a job working in franchise organizations, yet most do not know they're working for franchisees who are often local owners. Global franchising contributes over a trillion dollars to the U.S. economy and that's a tremendous economic impact from only a few thousand companies," Jennifer states.

Kushell did get an opportunity to work with her mentor Fred DeLuca's company. She created the Subway Global Challenge that engaged young people in 100 countries. Then, they built the NextGen in Franchising Campaign, which continues today. The competition inspires and empowers young people with businesses that can scale through franchising to learn from the best in the business. She is also excited about social franchising—a triple bottom-line business model that ties traditional business with cause-related activities to produce social benefits and outcomes. Identifying young new concepts like this from around the world was one of the most exciting outcomes of this program.

"One winning entry was a social impact franchise started by an American and Ugandan building water filtration systems and premium drinking water franchises," Jennifer shares. That exposure from winning the NextGen competition, helped JIBU Water raise millions of dollars and enlist the help and support of experienced franchisors to build their franchise model.

Jennifer reminds us of the popular saying in the franchise community: Franchising is like being in business for yourself, but not by yourself. "You're building on top of the hard work of other people. You're leveraging the time, money and proprietary systems used to operationalize a concept, replicate and scale it—to provide you with an opportunity to build a more viable start-up. That's a really great opportunity for a lot of people who are not comfortable with raw entrepreneurship, in which you often start something from scratch with everything unknown. Franchising is a better model for so many."

Jennifer's advice to would-be franchisees is to take time to really investigate the companies you are considering working with before making an investment. From reading all the documentation, agreements and published reports, to leveraging experts to help you evaluate your options, potential franchisees should surround themselves with quality information and professional expertise every step of the way. "There are no guarantees," Jennifer cautions, "but there are lots of reporting requirements in place to make sure you're given a comprehensive picture of the franchise systems you may be investing in. You have a right to know what's working and what isn't, where the model isn't working and where the model is successful. You need to be asking those questions yourself, especially to other franchisees. I feel like 15-year-old me when I say it, but you must do your homework and you must do it well. It's as simple as that."

As a best-selling author and lifelong entrepreneur, Jennifer encourages anyone at any age who is considering franchising to embrace the idea of stepping beyond what we know and see. "I think it's really game changing to look objectively at our comfort zones and examine what's holding us back from getting to that next level. What's keeping us from meeting those new people, from trying that new job, from exploring that new opportunity, from finally being our own boss." Even Fred once said, it was only from seeing others who were bigger and more advanced that he knew he too could do it!

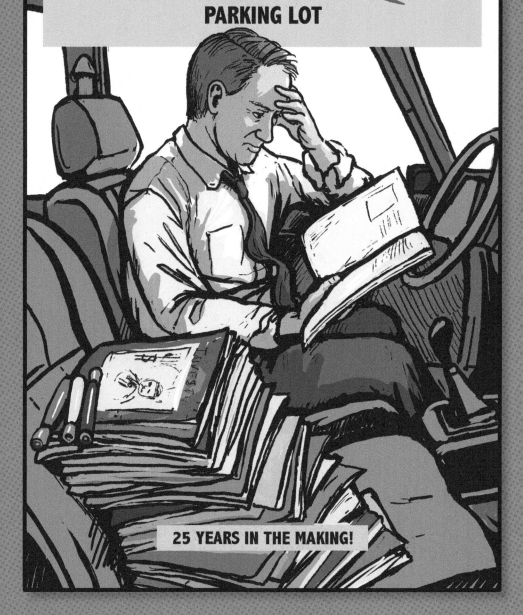

CHAPTER 3:
PREPARING FOR THE HUNT

A s a business leader, your ability to clear the clutter from your desk and your mind is a critical skill. It helps you be more focused and make the best possible decisions. Whether you're selecting the right opportunity from millions of franchise options, navigating a business deal that could put a sizable piece of your net worth at risk or hoping to become a player in a game where some people don't have your best interests in mind—it's a serious business. This chapter will help you build and maintain a realistic franchise search perspective and avoid the confusion and disorientation potential franchisees often experience.

AKERS OF ADVICE: DON'T LET YOUR ZEE CHOOSE YOU!

With nearly 800,000 units, franchise operations employ over 3,000,000 people, with revenues approaching $1,000,000,000,000 (that's *one trillion dollars*), there is no shortage of franchise opportunities but there are a few things to consider as you begin your search.

I've spent most of my career in corporate America, making money for other people. Like most, I didn't choose my career, my career chose me. When I first entered the job market, I sent out resumes and hoped someone had the good sense to overlook my sparse qualifications, interview me and conclude that I'd be a good match for whatever menial tasks they needed performed. They made an offer I couldn't refuse because ... I didn't really have any choice. That's how it goes. Too often, careers choose people instead of purposefully driving the process that will dominate 2,080 hours a year for the next 40 years of their lives.

Over time, I gained the experience necessary to move into executive roles. As a corporate leader, I had both authority and a certain degree of autonomy. My title, the number of zeros on my paycheck, the number of people who reported to me, the freedom I had to set my schedule— continued to grow with every passing year. If I made my number, hit my goal, completed the project, for the most part, I was left alone to get the job done. Compared to the career challenges many people face, I had it pretty good.

I had earned the right to say "no." Any offer floated past me was no longer *an offer I couldn't refuse*. In fact, I was refusing most offers in favor of a work-life balance that allowed me to be engaged with my family and be present as my kids grew. I was there coaching, attending BBQs and birthday bashes, watching my little girls grow to womanhood and eventually start families of their own. I'd earned the right to choose the roles and type of work I'd accept and just as importantly, the right to refuse opportunities that came with hidden costs, mostly family time and my own self-respect. From the outside looking in, most people would think I'd made it, that I was living the American dream. The only problem was that they were dead wrong.

WHAT TO BUILD AND WHO MIGHT COME?

I was living my own version of *Groundhog Day*, waking up every day to relive it all again. Same stuff, different day. There had to be more to life. Right?

CHAPTER 3

The simple fact that you picked up this book leads me to believe you understand.

You understand the hollow space.

You've had that nagging feeling that no matter what you do, no matter what you achieve or how well you do your job—there's something missing.

For me, that nagging feeling became a fully formed voice. Being the movie lover that I am, that voice was of course, James Earl Jones (think *Field of Dreams* not Darth Vader). Even though I wasn't visited by shoeless-ghost baseballers from a by-gone era, the message was the same. *"Build it and they will come."* My problem however was much worse than Ray Kinsella's, the Iowa farmer who cleared his corn crops to make way for a baseball field—I didn't know what to build or who might come.

I was on the outside, *looking in on my own life.* It was like my life was a bus ride and I was a mere passenger letting someone else drive. Every once in a while, my life would pull into a bus stop and I'd look around wondering, "How did I get here?" Worse, I'd just get back on, passively surrendering to an unknown route.

Have you ever felt that way?

Are you waiting for the next stop or setting the course?
Are you making the best of what comes your way or designing your future?
Are you a passenger or the driver of your own life?

MISTER GORBACHEV BUILD THAT MICKEY DEES!

That pretty much sums up my state of mind in 1985, when I started my franchise search. Mikhail Gorbachev was taking the reins of the USSR, Cabbage Patch Kids were selling their way to $600 million a year, a good ribeye steak was running $3.89 and Blockbuster was revving up for its dizzying ascent to becoming America's neighborhood video store. While McDonald's, the greatest franchise system of all time, was in the process of converting Ray Kroc's first restaurant in Des Plaines, Illinois, into a franchise museum, I was sitting in my Nissan Sentra in Little Rock, Arkansas. Between sales calls for my corporate job, I glanced over to a stack of cheap business magazines on the passenger seat and right there and then I made a decision.

I knew I'd wanted to go out on my own for a long time, but it wasn't anything concrete. I didn't take the time to ask the *BIG question... HOW?* And I certainly hadn't addressed the bigger question, *WHEN?*

Sound familiar?

Change the names and dates and your story is probably very similar to mine. Like you, I was unsure as to which franchise options were available to me and what made one franchise deal better than another. I had a long list of other questions, not the least of which was learning how the money worked.

ZEN OR FUD?

Question: Was this my moment of ZEN, the point at which the entire universe opened up and revealed its secrets? Was I starting to get it, asking all the right questions and making all the right moves? Or was I about to meltdown in a pool of my own insecurities?

Unfortunate Answer: It was definitely the latter. This was my moment of FUD.

I was overwhelmed with *fear, uncertainty* and *doubt* (FUD). Even writing these words, I can feel it creeping back in. Would I be building my family's future or taking an ego trip and putting everything I've worked for in jeopardy? There in my car, on my break, I picked up one of those magazines and continued reading. One break became many.

Being a *sophisticated* business guy, I created a *sophisticated* ranking system consisting of three (not one, not two, but three) colored highlighters. Sitting there in my smokin' hot Sentra, marking opportunities as low (red), moderate (yellow), and you guessed it, high (green). My parking lot planning sessions stretched on and days soon became weeks.

Weeks became months and my collection of business magazines slowly consumed the passenger seat and worked their way into the back. Luckily my 1.5-liter muscle machine had fold down seats in the back, which made the hatchback area accessible. You get the idea.

Months became years.

Four presidents later, long after Gorbachev tore down that wall and hung out the closed for business sign on the USSR, the cost of a loaf of bread was approaching what I used to pay for a ribeye. Texas turmoil raged in the executive suite at Blockbuster. James Keyes, the former 7-Eleven CEO tapped to save the video giant was instead presiding over its bankruptcy.

Finally, in the lightning-fast blink-and-you'll-miss-it speed of 25 years, I became a bona fide franchise owner!

And you can too *(quarter-century waiting period optional).*

Today, I run a chain of highly profitable franchise outlets, across three states and two franchise brands, employ hundreds of great people and, best of all, I get to work alongside my wife and daughters every day. We are solidly profitable and have a growing and loyal base of customers, many of whom we've served for years and know by name.

We have plans for more.

EMBRACING EMBARRASSMENT

Regrets?

Not exactly, more like wonder.

I often wonder what I could have accomplished if I were able to turn 25 years of indecision into action.

What would I have created?

There was no way to know at the time but the most important thing I've learned is that I can help others succeed. Not because I did everything right the first time or never took a false step. Not because I went to an Ivy League school or even because I always knew what I wanted. I didn't.

My middle-aged know-how is valuable precisely *because* of my hesitation, *because* I made mistakes and some of them were whoppers. *Because* every lesson was hard won. Now, I simply can't stop myself from doing everything in my power to help others avoid the mistakes I've made—lend a hand or an ear to fresh franchisees trying to make their organizations go.

My work with other franchisees is a big part of what I do. Every year I meet with franchisees across the country, visit their businesses, meet their staffs and help them avoid the pitfalls, as well as capitalize on opportunities they might not see. I give talks to associations and gatherings. And I listen. FUD is alive and well among prospective franchisees—it's a concern of those just starting out and something that's hard to shake for those seeking to expand an established business.

Franchise operations can create the future of your dreams, but there will be times you'll feel that no one on planet Earth could possibly understand what you are going through.

I can.

I've been there.

And I'm here to help. One way to make your franchise search easier and more productive is to start with a disciplined perspective of franchise offers.

THE BIG IDEA: 5 RULES OF FRANCHISE PERSPECTIVE

There are 5 key points that will ensure you maintain your perspective and keep FUD at bay:

1. There Is ~~No~~ Going Back
2. Franchising Isn't for Everybody
3. Not All Franchises Are Created Equal
4. Prepare to be Involved — Show it
5. You Are Being Sold!

1. THERE IS ~~NO~~ GOING BACK

In some ways, my journey was easier than what you are about to face. I just ran a Google search on the term franchises and .8 seconds later, I had 60,000,000 results. Back in BC times, *before personal computers*, the stone-age 20th century, searching for franchise opportunities was in a word ... *limited*. What we'd consider basic data today simply wasn't available until you were well into the selection process. That's one of the reasons my decision took so long. I had no way to make a confident decision on something that would dramatically impact my life, my family and our future.

Be my own boss? *Sure!*

Call the shots? *You bet!*

Potentially put my entire net worth at risk. *What? Say again?*

Franchising is not without risk. That's probably why my memories are so vivid a quarter century later. But don't be ruled by fear. Your goal should be to thoroughly investigate, understand your options and decide what's right for you and the people you care about. Developing your franchise business is a step-by-step process, most of which does not involve any lasting commitment. You aren't on anyone's timetable but your own.

2. FRANCHISING ISN'T FOR EVERYBODY

Not everyone is wired to become a franchisee. So, this book doesn't
assume anything about you. We've just met, and my goal is to share the
reality of what it means to be a franchise owner—the good, the bad and
everything in between. It may be that the greatest value you get from reading these pages is deciding that franchising isn't for you.

Yes or No.

Go or No Go.

One thing is for sure, making the right decision, whatever you decide, will
save you time, money and aggravation. If it's not your thing, the earlier you
realize it the better. If owning a franchise operation is what you were born
to do, the sooner you can confidently move forward, the better.

3. NOT ALL FRANCHISE OPPORTUNITIES ARE CREATED EQUAL

As you consider if franchising is for you, it's important to understand what
franchise opportunities are not. Franchise opportunities are not all created
equal. Some are better than others and some are better for who you
are, what you want and how you operate. Established brands may seem
safer but cost more. Newer franchises may make far fewer demands and
require much less cash, but today's hot brand, ANY brand, could potentially
go the way of Blockbuster.

The purpose of conducting your franchise search is finding a combination of *risk* and *reward* that you can live with. I mean that literally because

you will *live* with your decision, every day. Like a good pair of shoes, your comfort level is essential. The more you feel at home with the business model—what's expected of you, the level of support you'll receive, and the franchise folks you'll work with—better your prospects. If your *spider-sense* is tingling and something is telling you to *run*, then *run*. With all the franchise opportunities available, there is no need to accept something that doesn't feel right.

4. BE PREPARED TO BE INVOLVED

I was working with a would-be franchisee that had a playful streak and a strange sense of humor. We'd just had *the talk*, that's what Jeff and I call it when we sit down with a prospective ZEE to tell them there *is no Santa Claus*—that franchise-in-a-box opportunities are unicorn-rare, only operate in Area 51 and Big Foot already owns all the unit licenses. A week later, he showed up at my office to share some big news!

"You are wrong!" He declared, beaming with a cat-that-ate-the-canary grin.

"I've found a unicorn. A real franchise-in-a-box opportunity that won't take up any of my time," he continued.

"Ok, I'll bite. Tell me about it," I said, waiting for the punchline.

"It's a *vending machine* franchise, get it. It's a business that is *literally* in-a-box and all I have to do is sign the papers and the business runs itself!"

The look on his face told me he was only half joking. Sure, he was excited to find an opportunity that seemed to disprove my warning, but he was serious about his belief that he wouldn't have to spend time in the business. He'd incorrectly equated vending machine automation with business model automation—*there's no such thing*. So, I gave him the laugh he'd worked so hard for and then used the opportunity to reinforce what I'd said during *the talk*.

"How many sites does it come with?" I asked.

"Sites? What do you mean?" He replied.

"Did they give you a map of where each of the machines go?" I said, trying to contain a rapidly developing grin of my own.

"Well, um. They gave me this," he said, as he held up a photocopied map. "This is my territory and I'm the only one that can put the vending machines in this area."

"So, you have to figure out where to put the machines, right?"

"Uh, yeah," he said, the seeds of realization beginning to germinate.

"Did they give you a list of all the property owners, or will you need to figure out that on your own?"

Blank stare.

"So, you'll need to make appointments to visit with the owners and convince them to let you place the machines on their property, right?"

Blushing silence.

"Based on the projections the ZOR provided, how many machines will you need to have in operation to make a profit?" I asked. It was like taking candy from a baby (a baby vending machine franchisee).

"I haven't got that far yet, the exact number I mean, but they said it would take about 18 months to set-up my territory."

"So, this unicorn, this hands-free franchise-in-a-box you found will take about 18 months to open? That's one hell of a box!" Then, I slowly closed my hand into a knuckles-down fist, held it out in the space between us, looked him straight in the eye and opened my hand—*dropping the proverbial mic*. I didn't spend 25 years overthinking my franchise decision, without having learned a few things.

After a pregnant pause that had to have lasted two trimesters, he erupted in a burst of nervous laughter. He's a playful guy that appreciated my attempt at humor. He understood that my theatrics were intended to make an impression, to help him avoid the pain of having to live with a reality born from half-baked assumptions. I don't take pleasure in being right but it's a heck of a lot more fun than being wrong—and a lot less costly.

10 Universal Assembly Experiences (Furniture and Franchises)

 Looks great in the catalog and seems easy to put together

Comes in heavy boxes, so a lot of assembly is required

 Tempted to start building before you've thoroughly read the instructions

Reading the instructions is more confusing

 Spending time scratching your head, convinced critical pieces are missing

Find the large pieces that certainly weren't there

 Complete assembly incorrectly, disassembling most of what you built

Encounter DBEs (drive-by-experts), people that will impart unsolicited advice

 Once correctly assembled, the instructions suddenly make perfect sense

Discover leftover pieces. Spare parts or the result of something you did wrong?

Of course, assembly is just the beginning but there's nothing harder than the first step. Getting your bookshelf to stand on its own isn't the end-game. Your bookshelf has to bear the weight of your books and knick-knacks, withstand the dings and dents of everyday use and survive a few moves along the way. When the day comes for you to expand, to add new bookshelves, you'll tackle the effort with the confidence and speed that only comes from experience.

We've invested some time to convince you of a few things, while you are on your way to the trash, dispensing with the false notion that franchises are readymade businesses-in-a-box, you might as well throw out the notion that your new business is something you can set-up and walk away from. Rarely, if ever (so tempted to say never), does a business thrive without the active involvement of a dedicated owner. This doesn't mean you have to physically show up and work the register every day, but you do have to be actively and visibly engaged.

Businesses are like people; they need time and attention to thrive. As the undisputed leader of your organization, what you do and don't do, what you care about and what you let slide, set the tone for your business. It's up to you. Disinterested and disengaged leadership breeds lethargic, low-performing organizations. Owners that show their love and passion for the business, give permission for their teams to do the same.

I've met lots of people over the years and I'm sure I've generated all sorts of opinions about who I am (hopefully most are positive), but I can tell you one thing for sure: Anyone who knows me, knows that I love my business. *I love it.* I expect every member of our organization to care about our customers and each other. Not because I say so, but because *I show so!*

5. YOU ARE BEING SOLD!

Have Have no illusions, franchising is a *big* business and not just at the cash register. Much of the nearly one-trillion dollars franchisees take in each year is brand-generated. If a customer is in the mood for a Big Mac, *only* McDonald's will do, but *any* McDonald's will do. It's the power of the brand at work, and the better the brand the more valuable the franchise license.

Because the ZOR has already done the work of creating, establishing and promoting the brand, you'll be expected to share a portion of what you earn with your new business partner. Franchise fees, co-op marketing contributions and percentage of sales revenue are common components of franchise agreements and they can add up to *big* money. That's one of the many reasons you need to do your homework upfront.

That's why I suggest that you don't contact ZORs until you've done your homework, understand the basic outline of the business model and talk to a few franchise operators directly.

Once you've reached out to the ZOR of your choice, your search will transform into a mutual qualification process. While you are evaluating the franchise opportunity, the ZOR will be evaluating you.

Are you serious?

Do you have the financial means to make a go of it?

The better and more successful the franchise operation, the more they can demand of potential franchisees. A higher price and lots of qualifications and requirements may be hard work, but once you've become an owner-operator, that same screening process will help ensure the brand (the brand that you now have a financial stake in) isn't damaged by unprepared or underfunded franchise operators.

Franchising has become so commonplace, it's just not likely there's *a* franchise on every corner, it's more likely there are several. As a prospective franchise owner, the challenge won't be finding franchise opportunities, it will be sorting through all the franchise opportunities you find to select the one that's right for you *(see Chapter 4: Narrowing Your Selection).*

While ZORs have a lot to offer and can be the best business partners you could ever hope for, they are in the business of selling franchises and you should always keep that in the back of your mind. Slick marketing materials, and even slicker franchise representatives, need people like you to buy into what they're selling. Without you, the best built brands won't have the financial support, market presence or delivery capability to operate. It is a big business with big rewards, much of which depends on the revenues you'll help generate. Finding the right franchisor is just as important as finding the right franchise model.

Too often, our fears, lack of self-confidence, trusting nature and naiveté allow prospective franchisees to simply be swept along in a process they don't fully understand. Armed with the first draft of your *personal story*, the beginnings of your *people plan* and a firm *perspective on what franchising is and is not*, it's now time to begin the process of finding the franchise that's right for you.

SPOTLIGHT: THE ADVOCATE, MATT HALLER

President and CEO of the International Franchise Association (IFA), Matt Haller describes franchising as controlling your own destiny. In his role, Haller leads the charge in Washington, D.C., to protect the franchise business model on behalf of the franchisors, franchisees and suppliers that make up the IFA's nearly 1,000-member organization. "We have such an incredible story to tell," he shares. But don't call franchising an industry, rather Matt views franchising as a collection of industries that use franchising as a growth strategy.

Like Jerry, Matt doesn't sugarcoat the reality that franchising is a lot of work and definitely not a get-rich-quick scheme or business-in-a-box that's going to run itself. Matt suggests that great ZEEs are not generally the type of people who would start a business from scratch. They are people imbued with an entrepreneurial drive and a willingness to work within the systems and processes ZORs provide. For these folks, franchising is the most accessible means to develop opportunity. "Franchising is for people in any stage of their career and from any walk of life. If you have the wherewithal and access to capital, you can go into this sector and do quite well," Matt explains.

With one in ten members based outside of the U.S., franchising has a global reach. Eighty percent of U.S.-based IFA members have existing operations overseas or across the border in Canada and Mexico. "Every spot on the globe now has some imprint of franchising," Matt adds.

For over sixty years, the IFA has been a model for other countries to help them create a regulatory infrastructure that protects franchise brands and individual owner-operators. "In the early days of franchising, there were companies that were doing things the right way—and there were others that were not doing things the right way. The ones doing it the wrong way were selling concepts with no infrastructure to individuals that thought they were buying much more. We worked with the Federal Trade Commission and created a regulatory infrastructure that would protect brands and ensure prospective investors have a realistic understanding of what they were getting into. That's what became the nexus for the Franchise Disclosure Agreement."

Communication between franchisees and franchisors is key, according to Matt, who's a firm believer in the power and value of transparency. "It's like a marriage, right? There's going to be a little bit of give and take."

Matt and his team harness the voices of hundreds of thousands of franchisees, franchisors and suppliers to promote franchise interests and enlist the support of policy makers. Jerry is a long time IFA member and currently serves on the IFA's Board of Directors. "Jerry is an incredible teacher and I think somebody that has built an incredible business with a great brand. People can learn a lot from that experience," says Matt. "I can't think of a person that's done better in franchising."

"With franchising, you go into business for yourself but not by yourself. That's the strength of the model. That you aren't in it alone, that there's a team of people there to support you, as well as tens, hundreds, thousands of others, in other franchise systems, that are literally doing the same thing that you're doing. It's a built-in network of peer support. It's just an incredible resource," Matt adds.

CINEMA Z
SCALING A MOUNTAIN OF CHOICE.
BATTLING NUMBERS OF UNUSUALLY LARGE SIZE.
FACING THE SMALL BUSINESS CHALLENGE.
A NEW FRANCHISE OPPORTUNITY
THE PRINCE'S GUIDE
IT'S AS PROFITABLE AS YOU MAKE IT.

CHAPTER 4:
NARROWING YOUR SELECTION

Sifting through a massive number of franchise opportunities to discover *the one* that's right for you is *hard work*. It *takes time*. How much work and how long it takes is not a fixed formula. That's why Jerry created the SORT Method (*Search, Organize, Rank* and *Test*) to make the process simpler, quicker and more effective. In this chapter, you'll learn how to conduct a productive franchise opportunity search using Jerry's highly regarded SORT Method.

AKERS OF ADVICE: DON'T LET YOUR ZEE CHOOSE YOU

I remember the day I became a grandfather. As wonderful as the experience was, *Grandfatherhood* meant adjusting to a new role, a new stage in my life. It meant that people would look at me differently. Others would look at me based on what they believed grandfathers should be and how grandparents should act. In a way, it's the same process as becoming a business owner.

We think of business owners differently. There's a big difference between saying "I work for" and uttering the words "I own my own business." People will look at you differently and expect you to act differently. A whole new group of people will look at you like no one's ever looked at you before …

your employees. These won't always be looks of admiration. As you move through the process, you'll see judgment, disappointment, derision and even sympathy in those eyes. It comes with the territory. Just like joining the ranks of grandparents in the senior sect, the trick is to prepare your-self—to decide what being a grandfather or business owner means to you.

For me, the adjustment was a mixture of ego and fear. I was far too youthful to be a granddad and I wasn't ready to act like one, so I broke (my daughters say, shattered) the mold as you'll likely break a mold or two as you grow your own business. People like us, entrepreneurs, go fast and break things. It's part of what gives us the courage to do what others only dream about—in other words, it's in our DNA.

Be warned however, some things won't bend to your will, some things are so fundamental it's better to change your thinking than try to move the immovable. Finding the balance between what you are contractually, *legally obligated* to do under your franchise agreement, and what you *want to do* as an independent business owner is just part of a long list of immovables that won't bend to your will. Adjusting your thinking to account for the *Law of Business Numbers* is your first challenge.

Before I was a grandfather, I was a grandson, one of many grandkids that populated our family farm. Before cable TV, *People* magazine and social media, my family was my world. They were the stars of every show, the cover of every magazine and the subject of all gossip. My grandfather delighted in reminding us how good we had it. Yeah, he was an *"in-my-day"* kind of grandparent. He'd tell us tales of how he'd work six months to earn a nickel and with that nickel he could take a girl to the movies, buy some popcorn and a pop, and rest easy knowing that he'd still have some change in his pocket when it was all over. Back then we thought becoming a millionaire was the gold standard. If you'd amassed a thousand, thousand dollars, you'd reached the point of ultimate financial safety. You were set, could weather any storm and live out your days without any worries or cares.

Today, billionaires set the mark for mega-riches and if you want to rest easy on your movie date, you'll need a few pictures of Alexander Hamilton in your billfold. What was once *all the money in the world* won't pay for a week's groceries. Once unimaginable wealth has become an attainable target for a middle-class retiree.

It happens gradually. When we fail to adjust with the times, our perspectives become the stuff of loving mockery. We are perceived to be just like grandpa when he told us all what he could buy for a nickel.

Having to adjust to economic realities and evolving notions of value isn't new. What is new however is what we've never before faced—coming to grips with the numbers themselves. We live in a world of access, populated by incomprehensible numbers, big data and more data than a human could ever process. In the past we could operate without really having an understanding of the numbers themselves. Back then, understanding a nickel, a dime or a dollar was doable.

One. Two. Three. Four. Five.

Got it.

A million dollars may not be what it used to be, but have we ever really understood what a million anything is?

Or even a hundred thousand?

These are really big numbers.

Today, for someone planning a 20-year retirement, a million dollars in the bank isn't a million dollars—it's the reality of living on about $800 a week (after taxes) for the rest of your life! A king's ransom would be a movie that costs a nickel but is progressively less attractive as costs increase. Making the right calculation and taking the right steps now can help ensure your financial future. Missteps and miscalculations carry a different set of consequences.

Grandpa's mind-boggling ability to stretch a nickel isn't remotely as difficult as making that nickel last a lifetime. Finding franchise opportunities that check all of your boxes isn't remotely as challenging as selecting *the* franchise opportunity that you can profitably operate for years, decades or the rest of your life.

Whether you've managed a large financial portfolio, a modest nest egg or you've been living paycheck to paycheck—financial planning is *complex, emotional* and *terribly important*. Selecting the right franchise opportunity is *no less complex,* may be *emotional* and is one of the *most important business decisions you'll ever make!* But you can dramatically increase your chances for success by following Grandad's lead. Don't be in a hurry to make your selection, move purposefully from the large number of franchise opportunities to a few that seem to fit, arrive at *the* one that's right for you and *squeeze every cent of value out of the process.* Take your time, stay focused and be disciplined in your search and evaluation process.

How do you ensure you are making the best possible decision for you and your family? Over the years, I read everything I could get my hands on—anything that would help me understand my choices. Slowly, I began to see patterns, to identify specific aspects of franchise opportunities that I either wanted or wanted to avoid and developed a super-duper, high-tech system of using felt tip highlighters to color code the stacks of files, magazines and lists I'd accumulated. I then started the long and laborious task of sorting through all of those options. I soon expanded my technology platform to include a yellow legal pad and a very large accordion file.

Today, we have better options, digital tools that can help you do in an afternoon what might have taken a year to accomplish a few decades before. In this chapter, we'll share the simple but effective system we've created to help you get and stay organized and efficient throughout your franchise evaluation journey. You'll start with a simple spreadsheet and begin building it around your parameters and add interesting franchise options as you find them in your research.

Sure, the process may simply be the modern version of my old highlighters, legal pads and accordion files, but there is no replacing the ability to quickly collect and analyze franchise data the SORT approach provides. Simply put, data collection and analysis are the most important steps in the process, the steps you should spend the most time on and the steps too many potential franchisees rush through or skip entirely. In my experience, these folks generally pay a high price for doing so. Research and evaluation are the foundation of everything that follows. The house built on a poor foundation is rarely a good investment.

When I started the internet was just getting up and running, searching then was nothing like the search capabilities of today. Instead, I read thousands of books and articles, and none offered a systematic, step-by-step process to help make an objective decision. So, I created the SORT method of franchise evaluation for an audience of one—me! SORT helped me leverage the power of modern internet search capabilities, organize my findings, filter out opportunities that didn't match my criteria and make better decisions. As it turned out, I hadn't been indecisive, I'd simply lacked the tools necessary to validate my choices. SORT helped end my decades-long search in just a few months, and the best part was that I felt confident with my choice once I'd made it. No regrets, then or now.

Give this chapter thoughtful consideration. Read it twice. The entire chapter is an activity. Don't read or listen passively. Do the work discussed and you'll reap the dividends.

THE BIG IDEA: *SORT* METHOD

How long should your franchise selection process take?

Only you can determine that.

One thing we do know is you probably don't want to follow Jerry's example and let your selection process stretch out for years. We also know that a quick, knee-jerk decision could lock you into a bad situation for decades. Your challenge is to balance decision rigor against the reality that there are no perfect franchise opportunities. That's one of the reasons it took Jerry so long to make his franchise decision and why he drew on his past struggles to create a process that makes franchise search and selection faster, easier and more effective.

If you haven't done so before, open a browser on your computer or mobile device and type in a search for *franchise opportunities*. What's the number of results you received? When we hit the return button, our search results topped 60 million! That's a big number, so big, that it could easily justify the length of Jerry's 25-year search. REALLY!

Let's run the numbers.

Length of Jerry's (embarrassingly long) search: 25 years

Days in a year: 365

Total number of days Jerry searched: 9,125

Now if he reviewed each franchise search result manually, Jerry would have had to evaluate 6,575 prospects per day, every day, seven days a week, 52 weeks a year for 25 years to examine 60 million opportunities.

Sure, there are far more search results than actual franchise opportunities. That's because there are likely several hundred, sometimes thousands of links associated with a single franchise system (think McDonald's). Whether the number is 60 million or 500,000, the process can be overwhelming and it's likely you're not prepared to spend years finding the perfect opportunity. You need a way to speed up the process.

Jerry wasn't unwilling or incapable of making a decision. He's always known what he wanted. He was ready on day one, that's why he started the process. What held him back, what caused a quarter-century of indecision and anxiety was—*lack of process.*

In one of our early interviews for the book, Jerry recalled the experience:

"I was about to make the biggest financial and emotional bet I'd ever made. A decision that meant committing my entire life savings and putting my ability

to provide for my family at-risk, and even that wasn't the real issue. I couldn't come to grips with what I didn't know. I needed to be sure I'd done enough research, asked enough questions and considered every single angle. I got stuck in the gap between action and inaction, in the space between business owner and franchise looky-loo. My manual process wasn't a process at all. What I was doing only ensured I'd never catch-up, because the numbers of franchise opportunities were growing faster than my ability to evaluate them. I came to this realization right around the time we started thinking differently about the internet—when it was evolving into the powerful tool it is today. That's when I transformed my manual process into a scalable system. My decision didn't seem so hard after that, and within months I was on my way."

The SORT Method will help you conduct a *Smart Search* to ensure you won't get lost in the large numbers of opportunities available. You'll learn to *Organize Opportunities* that you find into manageable lists, each with benefits and drawbacks you need to consider, and *Rank and Test* your choices to reduce your search to a manageable few. Finally, *select* the franchise that's right for you! Take the SORT system seriously and you'll be prepared to make an informed decision and have confidence in the decision you've made.

SEARCH SMART

If you want to make better decisions, start by asking better questions. As a parent, I learned that asking the question, "Did you clean up your room?" will yield less dependable answers than when I asked, "Did you clean up your room, today?" The only difference between the two questions is the word, today, and that one word can make all the difference in getting the answer you want. In my kid's case, it may not have been the answer I wanted but it helped ensure I was getting a response to what I was really asking.

KEYWORDS

The same is true with internet search engines. Including keywords, like today, will not only improve the quality of your results but will also dramatically narrow the number of results you'll have to work with. For example, I just entered a generic franchise opportunity search and received 152,000,000 results. Changing my search to *franchise opportunities in California* reduced the number of results 85% (22,000,000), only a glimpse of the power you can harness for your own search.

SEARCH STRINGS

Using keywords in combination is called a search string. To extend our example, *franchise opportunities in California* is good, but *franchise opportunities in Bakersfield, California* for someone who wants to set up operations there is better. Any time you spend creating your search string will be repaid in the time you save later in the process. Try to get in the habit of documenting your search strings, adding and removing search terms as you develop your search criteria.

Let's smarten up your search string by including elements like:

GEOGRAPHY

Location is a great place to start because it's often a factor that will not change. It's common for people to start looking for opportunities in a specific industry only to discover other considerations are more important. Then you can change those search parameters, but your willingness to move is more predictable. If you are looking to start a local business, you don't need to review franchise opportunities that aren't available where you live. Adding a geographic boundary or even zip codes will narrow your search some, however you're just starting.

COST

While While geography and availability will make your searches smarter, setting financial limits will help you slice and dice your results in a big way. You may already know how much you are willing to invest in your new business. Let's say your limit is $100,000. A search for *"Franchise opportunities with available licenses in Dayton, Ohio, under $100,000"* will be a far more manageable starting point.

Smart Searching will help you focus your time and energy on the franchise opportunity options that are more relevant to you. Keywords define specific requirements (things you want or don't want). Strings combine keywords into super powerful search capabilities. In the next sections you'll learn how to organize your franchise opportunity pipeline, conduct franchise site research and develop your criteria for evaluating franchise opportunities and super smart search strings!

ORGANIZE

Jotting down your search string in a notebook or on a scratchpad for later use may be all you need, but when it comes to keeping track of franchise opportunity data there's a better way. With the help of Jerry's SORT Method and any common spreadsheet program, you can quickly translate your search results into a list of relevant franchise opportunities and easily keep track of what you've learned. Spreadsheet programs like Microsoft *Excel*, Google *Sheets* and Apple *Numbers* are among the most commonly used programs and, of course, pen and paper still work just fine.

Let's start with a simple spreadsheet consisting of three columns:

1. Franchise Name
2. Web Address
3. Notes

THE DIRTY DOZEN

Start by filling in the first column of your new spreadsheet with the names of a dozen or so test franchise opportunities. In honor of Jerry's love of movie references, let's call your list *The Dirty Dozen*. The goal of the Dirty Dozen is to help you get and stay organized throughout the evaluation process. As you become familiar with the SORT Method and more comfortable and confident in your evaluations, your list is likely to grow as will the volume of information you'll need to manage. Don't underestimate this simple approach, as it can be the most powerful tool you have in the early part of the evaluation process and your best defense against the mounting data you'll accumulate as you progress.

Since you're reading this book, you've probably spent considerable time thinking about the possibility of becoming a franchise operator and it is also likely you have a few brands already in mind. So, for this exercise, select a dozen or so franchise brands you are willing to consider.

Can't think of a dozen?

No worries.

You can just pick a few of the franchises that operate in your neighborhood or conduct a quick web search for franchise opportunities in your area. When the results pop-up, scan the list for brands you are familiar with and have a positive (or at least neutral) opinion. This should give you more than enough candidates to complete your test list.

Don't pick brands that, for whatever reason, just don't do it for you. Maybe you are thinking about a fast-food opportunity and a familiar brand comes to mind, but you remember that your second cousin's, best friend's, kindergarten teacher ate there in 1974 and found a cockroach in her salad and now, every time you see that brand, you think about it. Dump it! One of the benefits of so many brand choices, you should, never, ever settle for anything less than your top picks!

Create your super simple, Dirty Dozen list. Don't worry too much about getting all the details into your spreadsheet right away. Instead, just enter three basic pieces of information to guide your initial exploration. Open your spreadsheet and type the following words in the first row of cells; Franchise Name, Website and Notes, that's it. These are your column headers.

1. Enter the 12 brands you selected in the first column of each row.
2. Find the web address for each of the franchise brands on your list and enter it into the second column.
3. Use the third column for notes, additional information or reminders.

If you aren't comfortable with spreadsheets that's okay, just use a handwritten list for this exercise and then find your people plan (Chapter 2 activity) and add, *"Someone to help me develop spreadsheet skills"* to your list.

VISITING FRANCHISE WEBSITES

Use the addresses you've found to visit the websites of each franchise on your list. Take a look around. How are the sites organized? Do the sites walk you through the process, or do you have to dig to understand the process? As you read, what questions come to mind? Go slowly and keep asking yourself, *"What would I need to know and do to move from this webpage to purchasing a franchise license?"*

Many of the top franchise sites offer clear information, starting with the availability of franchise territories, costs and financing. As you explore, make notes about what you see. Note the things you like, the things you don't like and the things you don't understand. Pay special attention to FAQ (Frequently Asked Questions) sections, noting the types of questions they include and the kinds of answers given. These are clues as to what drives the franchise-licensing conversation.

Along the way, you'll likely find your way to a section that says, "For more information, *Contact us*." In the franchising process completing a contact form indicates that you are an active prospect and it's almost certain the ZOR will reach out to you to begin formal contact; a process that takes the kind of preparation you're just starting to do in this chapter. Since we're early in the book and you are just getting a feel for how it all works, we'd strongly suggest you don't submit any contact information until you've completed this chapter and all of its associated activities.

RESEARCH REVIEW

After you've completed your research exercise, review the notes you entered into the spreadsheet and identify the topics you covered. Did you include notes on some topics more often than others? Did you come to learn that some topics are more important to you than others? These topics provide the earliest clues as to what's important to you. Together, they represent your initial evaluation criteria, the standards by which you'll decide what franchise is right for you.

Let's clarify this idea by examining an everyday example.

Victor's Vacation

Victor needs a vacation. It's a pretty big decision for Victor, so he jots down a few notes describing his ideal vacation:

"I'm thinking about a beach for sure! It needs to be warm and sunny. I want a REAL vacation, a full two weeks. I don't have a lot of money to spend. The only time I can get off work for two weeks is late January."

This brief set of vacation notes contains the criteria for Victor's vacation success:

Location: Beach
Temperature: Warm and Sunny
Length: Two weeks
Cost: Low budget
Timing: January

Victor can use his criteria to make the best possible vacation decision. Since Victor lives in upstate New York and wants to vacation in January, he'll likely have to travel south to find a warm and sunny beach. The further he goes, the longer it will take him to get there, reducing beach time. Distance may increase cost. Victor's vacation criteria alone don't mean he'll make the best decision. He needs to evaluate each requirement separately and in relation to one another, to rank and test his requirements.

ADDING CRITERIA

Applying the same process to your Dirty Dozen list, jot down a quick list of the topics you noted, paying special attention to the topics mentioned multiple times and those you feel are particularly important. Maybe you noted license availability, geography and finance (examples we used in our discussion of search strings).

Looking at your list, is there anything you could or should have added?

It's likely your list includes price, but what does that really mean, the cost of the franchise license, start-up and build-out costs or cost of operation? And what's the difference?

Did you consider phase of the brand's growth?

What about location (storefront, office or home)?

Did you note the number of licenses or territories you want or can afford?

Are you interested in new or existing units?

Do you know what industry you want to work in?

Did you note the role of the owner in each of the franchise systems you evaluated? *You should consider the owner's role because, depending on the model, that's likely going to be your job!*

How'd you do?

Chances are your list missed a few of these considerations. You may not even be sure what some of them really mean, so we've included an initial list of eight criteria you can use to evaluate which franchise opportunities may be right for you.

RANK AND TEST

Let's say we evaluated franchise opportunities A, B and C and noted that the franchise license fee was within our investment range. Cool! When do we open?

Looking more closely, we discovered the cost of building out the physical location of the franchise "B" was simply too high. Bye-bye opportunity B.

As we continued our research, we soon realized that the break-even projection for opportunity C—how long a franchise in that system typically operates before it starts generating more cash than it consumes—was way too long. See ya!

With B and C out of contention, opportunity A is looking good, but there's still a long way to go and using criteria to Rank and Test opportunities will help you stay in control of the entire process.

Franchise search criteria is unique, reflecting your goals and objectives, how you view your role in the business, your access to capital and tolerance for risk and any number of other criteria. To help you get started, we created a list with eight of the most common selection criteria: price, owner role, industry type, cost of operation, fast growth, home-based or mobile, unit options (single, territory or geography) and new or

PRICE (INITIAL INVESTMENT)

Price is a significant factor in any franchise decision. Cash is a limited resource, so the cost of your initial investment is a make-or-break issue. Being realistic about the amount you are willing to invest, and using that amount as a filter, is a great way to pare down your list quickly. But the initial investment is just part of the cost equation. The cost to open your new business also includes the money you'll need to build and prepare to open your business (which is often more expensive than the licensing fee), and the money you'll need to keep the business afloat in the early days, months, years of operation, until you start turning a profit.

OWNER ROLE: ACTIVE OR ABSENTEE

Some ZZORs expect their ZEEs to be actively engaged in day-to-day business operations, others have no problem with absentee ownership. The active owner was a central component of traditional franchise models. Traditional thinking suggested that active owners would be more engaged in their businesses than absentee owners, pay more attention to the needs of the local community and respond more quickly to local market changes.

From a practical standpoint, as an active owner you may find yourself making sandwiches, frying chicken or otherwise working on the frontlines of your business. If you are the hands-on type, this role was made for you. Active or absentee, your choice may impact your future growth options. As an active owner, your ZOR may not allow you to own more than one location.

Working with franchisees in many different models and under both actively engaged and absentee owners, we have found one common denominator in successful franchise owners in both tracks—*engagement*!

Active or absentee, extraordinarily successful franchisees stay engaged. Absentee doesn't mean uninvolved. Successful absentee owners may not work the front counter, but they are intimately engaged in business strategy and planning. They make periodic (often unannounced) visits to the stores and take time to learn about their employees and customers. They demonstrate their interest, because if the owner doesn't care about the success of the business why will anyone else?

INDUSTRY TYPE

As you think about what you want and don't want, your first reaction may be to eliminate an entire category of franchises because you don't know anything about the industry. If Jerry had used those criteria, he would never have started his business.

"When I finally decided to become a franchise owner, I had BIG EYES and liked much of what I saw, except for the businesses themselves. The idea of owning a business was driving me. The idea of running a business in an industry that I knew nothing about scared the wits out of me. Fast food, business services, home repair—WHAT? I remember thinking to myself 'Are you crazy? You don't know anything about any of these industries!' Luckily, I have an incredibly supportive family, so when I told my wife what I was looking into and shared my enthusiasm for the whole idea, she said, 'Are you crazy? You don't know anything about these industries!' So, yeah, we got over that."

If you've been worried about your lack of expertise, or after the last section, you've just started worrying—don't. One of the best things about a solid franchise system is that you, as the owner, don't necessarily have to know anything about the technical side of the business.

While most of the franchise businesses are retail-oriented, there are some franchises that focus on business-to-business (B2B) products or services. For those who don't see themselves dealing with walk-in retail customers, B2B franchises offer a viable alternative.

B2Bs focused on products might sell office equipment or supplies. Service focused B2Bs might offer billing services, virtual technical support, sales and marketing project management, debt collection or any number of other services.

B2B franchises tend to have a predictable office experience, with predictable customer interactions. Transactions tend to be larger but fewer in number and less frequent. Fewer customers suggest lower staffing requirements. However, B2B franchisees often start out by assuming the active owner role, acting as salesperson or store manager, until the business can support additional staff.

Retail segments are more familiar, representing businesses most of us patronize regularly. Segments like fast food, hair care services, health food, auto repair, pet services and a host of other categories. Retail business interacts with more customers than B2B businesses, have much larger transaction volume and frequency, but a smaller transaction size. Once you get one retail location open and running successfully, it is easier to open another and continue to grow as opportunities allow. Retail profitability is sensitive to how well the organization is run, the scale of the business and how consistently it delivers the customer experience.

High levels of customer interactions and transaction volumes indicate the need for a larger workforce. High turnover among retail workers is the norm, requiring an ongoing recruitment effort. The steady flow of new hires requires a well-developed onboarding and training process.

The need for an operational footprint, a store or retail outlet, means retail business must be proactive in planning future growth, working with real estate brokers looking for future development sites, which entails a lengthy lease obligation. As retail businesses grow, the active owner role generally changes. The bigger the retail operation the more time you'll likely spend working on the business (paperwork, payroll, human resources, real estate, etc.) and less time working in the business (at the register or making sandwiches).

COST OF OPERATION

As you research various franchise options you will see terms like low cost, low investment. In our experience when something is described as low cost or low investment there is a reason for it. The reason may not be negative, but certainly something you need to be aware of and consider as you work through the process.

A franchise may be low cost or low investment because they are new and have little track record. The lack of a track record typically means more risk. Low-cost franchises often take more time, energy and ultimately money to get the business going in your market. New franchise offers are run by organizations that may still be developing their operating systems. Which means, you may not get the level of marketing and operations support and training that you'd receive from a more established offer. It will not be as built-out as the more established brands.

In addition, there are hidden costs that you might not see at first. Take for instance the cost of funding operations until the business is able to generate enough cash to pay for its own operation. This information is generally easy to find on the franchisor's website. You may start by looking at the Frequently Asked Questions (FAQs) section, which often includes a question like, "How long before I start to make money?" The longer it takes for the business to start producing enough cash to cover its own operation expenses, the longer you'll have to underwrite the cost of the business.

FAST GROWTH

The term fast growing generally refers to a franchise offer that satisfies a previously unaddressed need or niche that the market has quickly embraced. Fast growers often experience explosive, high-percentage growth, which may result from the small size of the ZOR. With over 30,000 global franchise locations, if McDonald's opened 300 new units, they'd post a whopping 1% growth—not exactly headline performance. However, if ACME franchise started 30 units and moved to 300 units quickly, ACME would be able to claim 1000% growth. It is not uncommon for smaller, newer franchises to promote growth reflecting a doubling or tripling of their business and that's a good time. What's important for you to remember is that past performance is no guarantee of future success. Today's hot franchise may be tomorrow's cold fish. Take notice of growth, and then dig deeper and monitor over time.

HOME BASED, MOBILE OR STOREFRONT

Home based, mobile or store front will be terms you will see constantly in your study of franchising. Home-based means that you can typically run the business from the comfort of your home as a startup. While convenient, home-based business may offer limited growth opportunities.

Jerry has a friend who has run a marketing franchise from his home for over a decade. He has a home office and occasionally uses his dining room table if he needs room to spread out. He is a one-man shop and probably always will be. He is happy with his business, wouldn't change a thing. Isn't that the point? Each of us must decide what independent business success means.

Mobile means the business can move and operate from anywhere. This could mean the business is not geographically limited, allowing you to move to another city and start up your business again simply by notifying the franchisor and paying a fee.

Examples of more mobile franchises include food carts and pet grooming services. Most mobile models work from wrapped trucks or trailers and bring their services or products to you at your home or special event or where people gather (parks, fairs, etc.). Mobile businesses are typically one-person businesses designed for people who are happy being their own boss and having some freedom.

Traditional storefront franchises typically operate out of a brick-and-mortar location. Strip centers along main business thoroughfares are the norm in this model. It could be a standalone building such as with fast food, a corner of a grocery store or big box store or attached to a larger retail building.

SINGLE UNIT, TERRITORY OR GEOGRAPHY

Many franchise systems allow and even encourage franchisees to operate more than one unit. Single unit ownership is a much different experience than running a territory or geography, in which you may help manage other franchisees on behalf of the ZOR. Territory and geographic opportunities tend to become a more corporate version of the franchise model. Instead of operating a single unit or a few units you own, you'd act on behalf of the ZOR to help develop the territory or geography, selling franchise licenses, training and managing the group of owners in your area.

In this franchise model, the ability to grow locations is limited only by the number defined by the franchisor agreement and your personal business goals.

Jerry's worked with people who have thrived in a franchise system where they were only responsible for one location and minimal staff, and others that turned their franchise territory into a big business. Hands-on people that enjoy interacting personally with their customers wouldn't be happy being stuck behind a desk, running a regional operation. Big dreamers and systems folks that love to build business operations may not enjoy having to work the front counter. It's not a matter of better or worse, it's a matter of what works for you. Find your fit!

NEW OR EXISTING OPERATION

One of the decisions you may face is whether to buy an existing franchise unit or open a brand-new location. You know by now that there is no better option, the choice all depends. A new business is a new business, you'll have to do, well, everything! It's risky starting a new business. Selecting an existing business has its own potential risks and rewards. On the one hand the business already exists—so you know it can work. On the other hand, you'll have to understand why the business is for sale.

Does it ever make sense to buy an existing franchise that's failing under poor management?

What if the business is a success but the owner wants to sell for reasons that have nothing to do with work?

Is buying a failing business at a discount better than buying a successful business at a premium?

Or is it a better bet to go with a shiny new operation?

When Jerry finally pulled the trigger to become a franchise owner, he and his wife Mickey examined an existing operation. They saw a struggling business that didn't have to be that way. A well-respected national brand operating in a market with enough demand to support the existing unit and potentially one or two more. Jerry and Mickey saw a structurally sound business in need of repair and attention. It was a risk, but they took on that struggling franchise because as Jerry put it:

"The existing business meant existing, immediate cash flow (new franchises will generally not break even for months or even years after the grand opening), a fully-experienced staff, established systems, name recognition and an established brand. For Mickey and me, it gave us a chance to test the waters before building our first new location from the ground floor. Of course, brand new franchise locations are spotless, and you will need limited or no

maintenance or updates for months or years. Your staff will all be hired and trained by you and they won't have to unlearn bad habits."

Returning to your spreadsheet, to the right of the information you've already been working with, add a new column for each of the criteria you distilled from your notes and any or all of the criteria we just discussed. Your SORT spreadsheet is quickly becoming a sophisticated evaluation tool, a framework to help you rank and test if franchise opportunities could be right for you.

The intersection between a row (franchise opportunity) and criteria columns creates a ranking cell, a place to note the quality of a franchise opportunity as it relates to specific criteria. Consider any or all of the following assessment and data categorization types:

Measurable Quantity. Using a simple 0–10 scale with 10 being best or most desirable. Deciding what's a 10 and what's a 0 all depends on you and what you think is important.

Binary Choice. Some criteria present only a binary choice, something that either is or is not. In these cases, use a yes/no for the column.

Case or Categorical. Ranking criteria based on class or categories (A, B, C, etc.) can be useful in organizing groups of opportunities.

Data Catch. Finally, there may be comparative data you'd like to capture. For example, the number of franchises in the system or the year the franchise started operation.

If you take the SORT approach seriously, you'll quickly come to two realizations:

First, there are many more things you need to consider than the list you distilled from your notes or the short list of criteria we covered.

- Do you have an industry preference?
- Would you rather run a fast-food restaurant or a picture framing service?
- Would you be just as happy running a hair salon as a juice bar?
- We've talked about price and cost of ongoing operations, but are there other costs you'd want to consider (*price of license, cost of build-out, royalty cost* and *more*)?
- What types of customers and employees do you want to work with?
- Would you rather sell services to businesspeople or serve meals to your neighbors?
- Would you rather work with auto mechanics or part-time college students and retirees?

Second, you aren't going to get all the information you need to make an informed decision all at once—it is a big job …

- It takes time, work and consideration to complete an evaluation.
- You will not be able to complete an evaluation in a single day.
- The information you need isn't available from a single source.
- No one person will have all the answers you need. Beware of anyone that suggests they have all the information you need, or they already know the franchise that's just perfect for you—they don't. How could they? You don't even know for sure what you want yet.
- You'll begin many evaluations but end up completing a handful. Why? Because the SORT criteria help you eliminate most opportunities before you needlessly invest time or money in opportunities that are not a good fit for you.
- Avoid shortcuts! Finding a slick way to download a list of 10,000 franchise search results into your spreadsheet using an app or browser extension may seem productive, but the approach isn't likely to

speed your efforts. When it comes to your list, remember the adage: Garbage in, garbage out! It is far more important for you to conduct thorough research on a small number of opportunities, to help build an appreciation for what matters most to you in the

ACTIVITY: QUICK SORT

Apply the SORT Method to your own franchise search. Using a spreadsheet application create your SORT evaluation form and you'll quickly narrow your search into a shortlist of well-qualified franchise opportunities.

Franchise ownership is a life-changing commitment for you and your family. Investing the time and attention necessary to make the best choice will have a dramatic impact on your chances of success or failure. We believe there is a great franchise fit for anyone willing to make the leap and put in the time necessary to find the right match. We have also seen exceptionally intelligent and skilled people fail because they made uninformed choices. So, ask questions. Learn by exploring. Take your time going through each website. Go slow now, so you can go fast and make a great decision when you are ready.

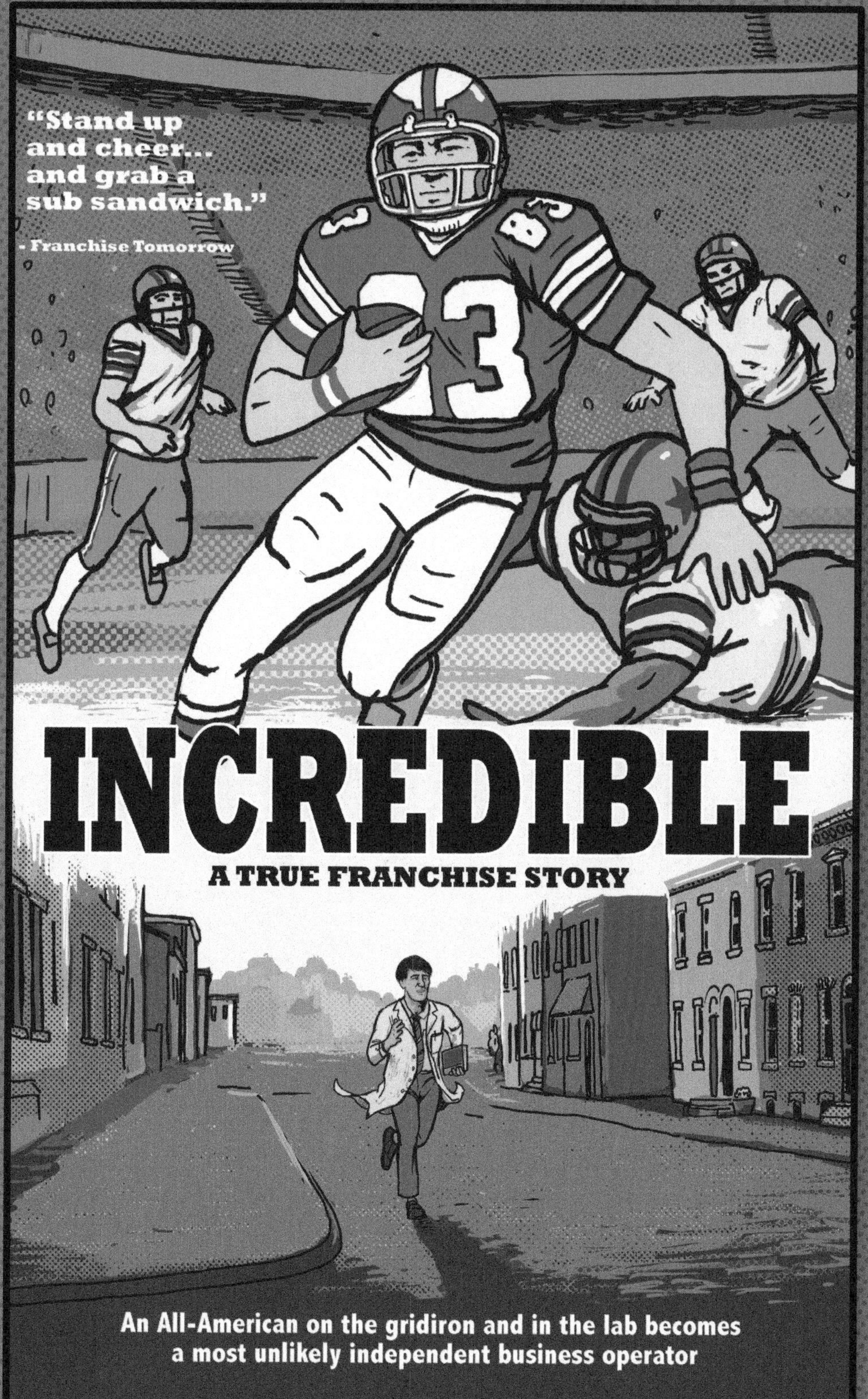
"Stand up and cheer... and grab a sub sandwich."
- Franchise Tomorrow
83
INCREDIBLE
A TRUE FRANCHISE STORY
An All-American on the gridiron and in the lab becomes a most unlikely independent business operator

CHAPTER 5:
MEETING YOUR NEW BUSINESS PARTNERS

nextricably linked, the ZOR–ZEE relationship is interdependent and mutually accountable. You will be as responsible to your franchisor as your franchisor is responsible to you. At once, business partner and vendor, ZORs are contractually bound business partners entitled to a share of every dollar the business generates and vendors that provide services and support (and in some cases products). So, while you'll operate an independent business, you won't be independent. Inevitable and undeniable, the interdependence of your business with its franchise parent can be either a source of strength or frustration. In this chapter, you'll learn how to get things moving in the right direction by preparing to meet with your new business partners. From first contact to your corporate visit, you'll learn what to expect and what to avoid.

AKERS OF ADVICE: PEOPLE FIRST

Franchisors are always looking for future Rock Star ZEEs! All models need a steady influx of driven franchisees who have the determination and wherewithal to grow a small business, and the potential to one day operate multiple units or entire geographies with a high level of success. The process starts with people.

The first step to ensuring your success is embracing the relationships that spring up along your journey. From your initial contact with a Franchise Broker or Franchise Development Representative to your formal corporate visit, the people you meet can either support your cause and speed you along or make the road more difficult. Imagine looking back after 10 or 20 years in the business and remembering the path you walked, the forks in the road that made all the difference. Wherever the franchise road takes you, the force behind every twist and turn will be the people you interact with. Providing you support you didn't realize you had or putting barriers that slow you down, people are the key.

I'm a member of multiple franchise organizations but I'll never forget my first experience and the first people that helped me along the way. Fifteen years later, I am still good friends with many of the people involved in my first franchise purchase, and I'm thankful for what I learned from every single one. After completing the preliminaries, my wife Mickey and I attended a formal corporate visit. We met with various department managers and even the president of the company. In a rapid-fire series of 30-minute meetings we asked questions, discussed fears, considered resources and eased our concerns about investing our life savings in a business that was entirely new to us.

Since then, I've spoken with thousands of franchise operators and I've learned that each person's journey from first meeting to securing a franchise license is like a snowflake—no two experiences are exactly alike. Industry type, prior experience, financial position, business goals, time of year, mood, personal style and your spoken and unspoken expectations (as well as those of the franchisor) will make your experience unique. Yet, all franchise journeys share one thing in common—people!

From your first meeting with a franchise representative to making your own corporate visit, the relationships you build along the way will set the tone of the entire process. Building strong, mutually supportive relationships will make everything that follows much easier. Failing to connect with those you'll be working with may create unnecessary tension, cause rifts and slow or stall the entire process. To ensure you make the best of the opportunity, do your homework—understand what to expect and what's expected of you.

It's like the Mark Wahlberg movie *Invincible*, which chronicled Vince Papale's journey to the NFL. Vince dreamed of playing for his hometown team, the Philadelphia Eagles. As a 30-year-old with minimal playing experience, Papale's prospects were infinitesimal. Undaunted, Vince caught the eye of Eagle's head coach Dick Vermeil and earned a tryout—this was his chance. He did everything he could to prepare. He sought advice from other players. He wore lighter quarterback pads, which allowed him to outrun competitors, and took unbelievably hard hits to prove his worth. He prepared mentally and physically and succeeded against the longest of odds. In 1976, Papale become the oldest rookie in the history of the NFL and went on to play in 41 games over three seasons. Voted Special Teams Captain by his teammates and *Eagle's Man of the Year* in 1978, Vince Papale is a great example of what, I believe, being a franchise operator is all about. While his talent won out in the end, it was the people along the way that made all the difference to Papale's success. The people that put in a good word with the coach. The people who shared performance secrets. The people who stood up to show their support. Success is a team activity.

Skill, determination and commitment are necessary components of franchise success, but the people you know and the relationships you build will determine what you are able to achieve.

THE BIG IDEA: RELATIONSHIPS, RELATIONSHIPS & RELATIONSHIPS

Franchisors need a steady influx of driven franchisees who have the commitment and wherewithal necessary to grow beyond one location and run several with a high level of success. As you begin to engage with franchise system representatives, remember you only get one chance to make a first impression.

Typically, the first person you'll interact with is the Franchise Development Representative or a Franchise Broker.

FRANCHISE DEVELOPMENT REPRESENTATIVE

Initially meeting with someone from the Franchise Development side of the business is common. Specialists in working with potential franchisees, Franchise Development personnel are there to help you navigate the process. They are also the gatekeepers between you and the people who will complete the licensing process. Do not make the mistake of dismissing this person because they are not high on the organizational ladder. They, too, have influence. Make a great first impression with the Franchise Development Representative assigned to your inquiry and word will spread through the system clearing obstacles and smoothing the way for your integration into the franchise family.

FRANCHISE BROKERS

Some ZORs employ Franchise Brokers to help them qualify prospective licensees. Brokers represent a portfolio or group of franchise offerings. Like Franchise Development Representatives, the broker's job is to answer questions, help get financing in order and pique the buyer's interest. Only after the brokers complete their work, will you begin working directly with the franchisor.

TAKE TIME TO CARE

Regardless of the title, your first personal contact takes your franchise journey to a whole new level. Moving from passive investigation to active pursuit, you'll be working with a stranger who has the power to influence your future success. Creating an open and honest relationship is not only the neighborly thing to do but it's a savvy move that is likely to help you and the person you are befriending. So, don't rush through the process without taking time to learn a little about the person you are working with. Showing interest in your representative or broker's background and personal history will not only accelerate the development of the relationship but it is also a sign of respect. Take time to show you care. Of course, you must be prepared to share some of your own background and history, nothing that would make you or your potential new friend uncomfortable. The point is to find common ground and to begin seeing one another as people and potential friends.

EVERYBODY WANTS SOMETHING

While personal relationships are critical to franchise success, keep in mind the professional role and motivations of those with whom you are interacting. These motivations may not be apparent. ZORs are in the business of selling franchise licenses, right? If that were true, our advice would be buyer beware and nothing more but it's not that simple. Selling franchise licenses isn't like buying a car. It's not a single transaction. It's more like getting married, after somehow getting connected, there's a courtship and a commitment ceremony—but that's just the beginning. The same is true with franchise agreements. The best franchisors will be more concerned about ensuring that you have the skills, determination and temperament to succeed than trying to get you to write a check. They will be evaluating your ability to work the system and work in the system. As one Franchisor put it, "We've built the business operation, we don't need franchisees to reinvent the wheel. We need intelligent, enthusiastic licensees that can follow directions and color inside the lines. When we meet a potential franchise operator, we're asking ourselves, how easy is it going to be to work with this person? Keeping the system going is hard enough, we don't want to take on ZEEs who are difficult to work with."

BE THE NEWBIE

One of the best ways to pique the interest of your initial franchise contact is to ask great questions. Makes sense. Sounds simple. Yet, in practice, many franchise prospects hesitate to ask about the things they don't know or understand. The truth is, when it comes to franchising, what you don't know can hurt you. ZORs interact with potential ZEEs regularly and they're looking for people that are ready and willing to learn the system. Asking questions is a clear indicator of your interest and willingness to learn. Warning bells and red flags fly, when franchise candidates set out to impress franchise personnel with what they know and all the changes they'll implement to make the system better. Be clear. Whatever experience you bring to the table, the people that run the franchise system you want to be a part of have forgotten more about their system than you'll ever know.

You've been a franchisee for another brand.

Hey, that's great.

You've run a Fortune 500 company.

Isn't that special!

As an independent business operator, you'll draw on all your life experience. Your time working in another franchise system or running a Fortune 500 will certainly help you in your new endeavor, but when it comes to franchise success no one knows more than your ZOR. From a purely mathematical perspective, you may be looking to open one or a few units, while the ZOR has the experience of helping dozens, or hundreds, or thousands or even tens of thousands of ZEEs become successful. They know what works and what does not work—all from real world experience.

Here's a simple fact. You will never, ever, again, know less about franchising (at least the franchise you are evaluating) than you do right now and that is a-okay. Don't try to hide the fact that you are a newbie. Use it!

At this early stage, asking questions is an indication of your intelligence and drive. If you don't ask questions now, if you don't take the time to learn early on, people may begin to assume you know things you don't.

There's a lot riding on the choice you are making, so break the cycle. Enter the classroom and grab a seat in the front row. Reset your default to raised hand and get the information you need to make informed decisions every step of the way.

WHAT QUESTIONS TO ASK

Assuming you are willing to follow our advice, you may now be asking yourself, "What kinds of questions should I be asking?" This is where you start, *Live It 2 Own It*. Push your thinking beyond the idea of running a franchise operation to the reality of running a franchise operation. We've created a series of questions that may get you thinking.

Considering a food model?

How will you get the food?
Who are my suppliers?
How often do deliveries come?
What are the rules surrounding handling food?

With these few examples, it wouldn't take much for you to extend the list. You may even think these questions are obvious but what about the less obvious questions?

REAL ESTATE

1. Can I just find a site to operate or do I need approval?
2. What makes one site better than another?
3. Do you have someone to help me find the right location?
4. What sort of support can I expect to get from you?
5. What tools do you have available to help me make the best decision? (Demographic reports, traffic studies, desirable co-tenants and anchors to draw clients to me)

6. I'm providing a service to other businesses. Do I even need a site?

For more information on real estate, see Chapter 6: Selecting Your Site.

FACILITIES

1. Who is my main contact for facilities questions?
2. Am I required to use certain vendors? And, if yes, for what?
3. Can I design my own space, or will you do that for me?

For more information regarding facilities, see Chapter 6: Selecting Your Site, Chapter 9: Opening Day, and Chapter 10: Operations.

RECRUITING AND TRAINING

1. What's the best way to staff my business?
2. Do you have a formal training program or is that something I'm supposed to do on my own?
3. Which tools and practices do you offer to help me attract employees?

For more information regarding recruiting and training, see Chapter 9: Opening Day and Chapter 10: Operations.

MARKETING

1. How does marketing work?
2. What do you do for national marketing and branding?
3. What support do you offer to me in making decisions about local marketing?
4. Do I have to spend a certain amount on advertising?
5. What's a marketing fund?
6. Does the marketing fund come out of franchise revenue split or is it a separate cost?

7. How are my marketing dollars distributed?

8. What percentage goes to overhead versus actual marketing spend?

For more information regarding marketing, see Chapter 8: Marketing, Promotion & You and Chapter 9: Opening Day.

OPERATIONS

1. Once I'm open, can I set my own hours of operation?

2. Can I use my own forms?

3. How do I report revenues? Do you audit me?

For more information regarding operations questions, see Chapter 9: Opening Day and Chapter 10: Operations.

Of course, these are just a few examples and depending on the type of franchise you are considering, the questions may not apply to you but the point stands—ask questions. The more questions you ask, the faster you'll learn what you need to know to make your independent business a success.

ACTIVITY: SAY WHAT, NOW?

You've heard the expression, "It's like drinking from a firehose" to describe situations in which people must process large amounts of information all at once. The process of becoming a franchise operator can feel like that. Having a well thought out set of questions will help keep you organized, focused and on track. The sample questions don't begin to cover what you'll need to know to successfully run your independent business. In this chapter activity you'll start to build your own list of questions, and it's all part of preparing for your first contact with your new partners. For this activity, write out (or type into a new tab in your SORT spreadsheet workbook) a list of 20 questions. You'll end up with a lot more, but this initial list will not only get you thinking but will become the place you document new questions as they arise.

SPOTLIGHT: THE PLAYER, DON DAVEY

Developing this book, we met with thousands of people. These pages reflect what we learned about the *process* of independent franchise operation. We also learned a great deal about the *people* who populate the franchise world—a group of amazing people who are accomplishing amazing things. Let's travel to Tampa, Florida to meet Don Davey.

Whatever you think of when you think about football players, franchisee superstar Don Davey breaks the mold. As savvy and intuitive off the gridiron as he is on it, Davey grew up in a home with a unique playbook. Don's ticket into the game wasn't size, stamina, grit or determination—although he has superhuman levels of each. In his home, good grades were a requirement.

No 'A'.

No play.

Period.

Scholarship first was a fixed rule for Don and his five siblings—all part of the discipline the children's Marine Corps father sought to instill.

"When my dad spoke, you listened."

Don listened.

Graduating as his school's top academic student and his state's football player of the year isn't typical. A highly prized college recruit, Davey stayed true to his academics-first upbringing, selecting the University of Wisconsin not for the school's athletic program (Go, Badgers!), but for the quality of the university's vaunted engineering school (Go, science!).

Don humbly characterized his college career, stating, "I did well at Wisconsin." A modest description for a student whose athletic performance earned him Big 10, All-Conference honors in his senior year. A modest description for a student whose academic record earned him All-American academic honors every year of his college career (1987–90). No Division 1 athlete, before or since, ever accomplished this feat.

Drafted 67th overall in the 1991 NFL draft, the Green Bay Packers called Don's name in the third round beginning his long professional football career. After four seasons with the Packers (1991–94), Don moved to Jacksonville (1995–98) where he played the remainder of his career with the Jacksonville Jaguars. While he was a professional athlete, the academic in him never left the scene. Don started to notice how other athletes thought about, or didn't think about, finances. He saw what he now calls "locker room" money. Young men with lots of money throwing it around like Halloween candy." Ever the engineer, Don designed a method of managing and growing his own finances—a method that paid dividends. "By my seventh season, I was financially independent and set myself up for life after football," says Don. Other players took note of Davey's financial savvy. So it wasn't surprising that when his football career ended, he traded the helmet and pads for a calculator and spreadsheets and became a financial planner. Superior performance soon followed as he sought new ways to expand his growing financial enterprise.

Looking to feed his independent and entrepreneurial spirit, independent business ownership seemed like a natural fit. "Franchising was appealing because it's like football. The franchisor hands you a playbook, a recipe for success, process, products, vendors and everything else. You follow this playbook, and you have a great chance to be successful," Don shares. He began a detailed search and found Firehouse Subs, an opportunity in his own backyard.

"Turns out, I actually knew the founders of Firehouse Subs, so I started digging in to see if this was a good fit," he says. Then, with only 20 restaurants in Florida, it looked like a company primed for rapid growth.

As attractive as the offer seemed, Don knew he had to do his homework before he'd feel comfortable with making the investment. After months of researching customer demographics, profit potential, locations, staffing, promotions and growth opportunity, Don signed a deal with Firehouse Subs for five restaurants.

On track to opening his first location, Don knew something was missing. Always a team player, Davey knew that he needed a team. He couldn't do it on his own and, more importantly, he didn't want to. The camaraderie of a team is what it's all about for Davey. "To be successful in football, you need a good team to help carry the ball over the goal line." Don needed a partner.

"There's this guy I'd hung out with a few times. His wife and my sister were good friends. He'd hit the glass ceiling in his corporate job and was feeling restless, so he was considering starting a franchise of his own. So I offered him a 20% share of the company to come work with me. It was the best decision I ever made."

The first store opening went great. So did the second. And the third. But opening the fourth store blindsided the new team. "We got cocky. We stumbled a bit and learned some lessons, but we forged ahead. It was a mediocre location, but we figured the great brand name would carry us through. It didn't, and it was a nightmare," says Don. They closed the restaurant and took their losses. Better for the lessons learned, they recovered and now operate 17 units in Orlando and other locations.

Do you have to be a world class athlete and academic to become a successful ZEE? Absolutely not (but it doesn't hurt). In fact, Don sought the help and support of others to help ensure the success of his operation. The process we are going through in this book isn't just about picking the right franchise for you, but helping you develop your own recipe for franchise success to understand what you are good at and what you might need help understanding or executing. Don satisfied his need to build and grow an independent business. "Being an entrepreneur gives you the ability to craft your own utopia. That's what I loved about it—creating something cool, going to work in shorts and T-shirts, surrounded by coworkers, partners [and] clients that they enjoy being around."

CHAPTER 6:
SELECTING YOUR SITE

n tthis chapter you'll learn why selecting the right site is one of the most important decisions you'll make as a franchise operator. *Akers of Advice* describes the importance of finding and securing the right location. *The Big Idea* then examines the site selection process, identifies the roles of the people involved and broadly defines some of the terminology commonly associated with commercial real estate development. Of course, the process differs among franchises. Some models, like home-based business, won't require any real estate development (if that's you, just skip to Chapter 7: Staffing & Talent Acquisition). For the rest of us, real estate development is a big part of getting our small business up and running.

AKERS OF ADVICE: A STALKER'S GUIDE TO SITE SELECTION

Finding the right location for your franchise business sounds easy—it isn't. You must correctly identify what your potential customers want and need today and in the future. You must understand current traffic patterns and anticipate changes. You'll need to accurately predict the prospects of the larger businesses (anchor tenants) that typically drive traffic to the property that feeds smaller businesses like yours.

There was a time when signing a long-term lease in a mall anchored by Circuit City, Blockbuster and Sears was an easy decision!

Times change.

Your willingness to test the waters, to see if you have what it takes to make it on your own, does not mean you are comfortable with high levels of uncertainty—few people are.

Each year, I'm asked to speak to thousands of ZEEs and real estate is the question I'm asked about most—it's my favorite aspect of franchise building. For me, it is absolutely fascinating to imagine my future customers, consider their lives, what they do each day, how they shop. How far will they travel to my new business? What will attract them to one shopping location instead of another? What will make us stand out from the competition?

Even afterward, after the signed lease or the property purchase, after the unit buildout and Opening Day, there's still the practical reality of cost. For most franchise operators, rent (or mortgage) and payroll expense are the highest monthly expenses. The one–two punch of property and people make real estate and staffing decisions critical. Of the two, personnel expenses are more controllable. In hard times you can trim staff, pick up shifts yourself to conserve cash, but your rent (or mortgage) is unchanging—each month, month after month, in good times and in bad.

QUICKDRAW'S BIG SURPRISE

A couple of years ago a franchisee (we'll call him Tim) sought my advice on improving a small group of fast-food franchises that he and a partner operated. Tim was ready to expand and wasn't sure about selecting a site. When Tim and his partner (let's call him Quickdraw) started their business, they'd purchased an existing franchise operation. So, even though they were experienced operators, this would be his first experience with site selection. As I talked with Tim, two things became apparent. First, the partners had not done the work necessary to make an informed decision. Secondly, Tim and Quickdraw were not communicating effectively.

I was working with Tim, trying to help him understand the fundamentals of commercial real estate, when the phone rang. It was Quickdraw calling with surprise news. He'd found a site and signed the paperwork on their behalf. Worse, Quickdraw didn't just commit their business to a ten-year lease, he'd BOUGHT the lot!

The RED FLAGS were flying!

In business, and especially among business partners, surprises are rarely a good thing. Quickdraw's actions were no exception. Unilateral decisions do not promote partner harmony. Buying property instead of leasing isn't just a business decision; it's a decision to start another business (real estate).

My mind raced ahead. If Tim was just learning about this, it was unlikely their franchisor knew either. While ZEEs are independent operators, ZORs have a legal interest in the business, and they play a big part in site selection. ZEEs are often contractually bound to get ZOR sign-off before securing a new location. The problems didn't stop there. Quickdraw's newly purchased property wasn't in a good location. Absent major changes to traffic patterns, demographics, zoning or other factors that could drive enough traffic to support the business, the location was a bust.

Quickdraw hadn't set out to sidestep Tim. Until this point, their partnership had been surprise-free. Later, Quickdraw explained that the commercial real estate agent he'd been working with made the recommendation—someone who should have known better. Someone that hadn't done the homework necessary to make such a recommendation.

What a mess. Tim and Quickdraw are still dealing with the fallout today. What's worse is the fact that the situation, setting out on the right path only to end up lost or in trouble, isn't unique or uncommon. No matter the depth of your franchise experience things will arise that you've never dealt with before. That's why we recommend that you go slowly. Ask lots of people a lot of questions. Seek and seriously consider the advice of professionals, and if you still don't understand, don't do it.

Every owner wants the best possible site for their new business to attract the maximum number of potential clients. That's why there's always competition for commercial real estate. Other franchisees and businesses are always looking for the best sites. That's why it takes time to find and secure the site that you want, and that meets the requirements of your franchise agreement.

We are often asked, "What makes the best location?" The answer is a firm "that all depends on the type of business you are going to operate." ZORs generally provide a detailed description of the ideal location. One of the more useful descriptions I've seen is:

> The best available location is in close proximity to a high volume 'daily or weekly visited' co-tenant or anchor tenant, with good visibility from the street, main entrance and/or parking lot.

Details matter because, next to selecting the franchise brand, choosing the right location for your new business is the most important decision you will make.

Don't worry. We are the first people to acknowledge the fear, uncertainty and doubt associated with franchise real estate—FUD. Our goal with you is twofold. First, to instill in you a sober respect for the importance of site selection. Secondly, to let you know that there's an entire support system you can use to help you make the right decision. From your ZOR to local real estate companies, from traffic and shopping analytics to the perspectives of other local business owners, to your own gut feeling and good judgement—there's a toolbox that will help you make the best decision possible.

THE BIG IDEA: SITE SELECTION TOOLKIT

In Chapter 3, we discussed the *5 Rules of Franchise Perspective*. The third rule—Not All Franchises Opportunities Are Created Equal—applies to site selection. Initially, you may think that selecting the site of your business is your decision. After all, you are the one who's going to sign the lease or buy the property, right? This is a great example of the unique relationship between ZOR and ZEE.

Yes, you'll have financial responsibility for the site but if you make a poor selection, your business may fail. When you fail, the entire system suffers. Unit failures may dissuade prospects from joining the system, other established franchisees may stop plans for expansion and the ZOR loses some or all of its share of the revenue the failed unit would have generated. Conversely, when a unit succeeds, the system benefits. It's not surprising then that franchisors have an interest in your site selection.

Because not all franchises are equal, the ways in which ZORs regulate and support site selection vary. Generally, ZORs staff a real estate function to assist and support franchisees in selecting the right site. In fact, most franchise agreements require site approval. So, while the financial responsibility is entirely yours, the decision is not. While your experience will differ, here's a high-level overview of the process.

PROCESS

Jerry often speaks about how fortunate he feels that his ZOR has an active, engaged and knowledgeable real estate department. The department includes regional experts that guide him and his colleagues in the selection of sites that are right for the area.

In the case of the franchisor without a real estate department, or more likely an ineffective real estate department, you will need to do much of the real estate research yourself. The cardinal rule? No one knows your market like you do. No one is taking the risk that you will be taking with this new enterprise. Do not abdicate the responsibility for real estate. It is your business and your decision. If you can't get the information you need to decide, go out and get it— build a D.I.Y. real estate team, drive the market and take the parking lot challenge.

D.I.Y. REAL ESTATE TEAM

Even some growing national brands cannot seem to grow their real estate department as fast as necessary to handle new franchisees. Knowing the basics of choosing real estate is critical for your success and necessary for you to build your own franchise real estate team. While Jerry enjoyed tremendous support from his franchise real estate team, he took the time to build personal relationships with local brokers. "They know our business and our longer-term goals. Together with the resources my franchisor provides, I've built an extended real estate team. Always on the lookout for a potential location that will meet our demographics, traffic patterns and plans for growth, the team gives us a running start, a little edge that's kept us at the front of the line for the prime commercial spots in our markets," Jerry explaines.

KEY PLAYERS

Site selection is a complex decision involving any number of variables and a host of experts each playing a unique role and each driven by a range of motivations. Your job is to meet these experts, understand their roles and motivations and then make an informed decision.

Important Note: *Federal, state and local laws and regulations change. Roles and titles differ among real estate companies. The legal meaning of the terms we discuss, and implications of real estate terminology may vary. The following sections offer broad descriptions based on our experience. Validate the roles, titles and functions of the people you work with and seek professional legal and financial advice before making real estate decisions.*

FRANCHISE REAL ESTATE REPRESENTATIVE

Most franchisors will have a real estate department and a set of tools to help you evaluate site suitability, often staffed by professionals with prior commercial real estate experience or people who have developed their careers around franchise real estate evaluation. Site selection is what they do every day. They'll reach out to regional or local brokers who monitor real estate inventories in their markets. Franchise real estate representatives will take the lead initially, walking you through decision-making guidelines.

As the process progresses, your franchise representative may provide you tools, research and data to help you analyze your market, identify your site selection sweet spot, the optimal mix of traffic count, co-tenant quality and draw, shopping patterns, demographics and other factors driving customer behavior. The franchise representative will also determine if the site you've selected meets the requirements of your franchise agreement and may assist you in your lease negotiations.

BROKERS (BUYER, SELLER)

As members of a regional or local real estate company specializing in commercial real estate including office space, shopping centers, strip malls, hotels, convenience stores and restaurants, brokers mediate the negotiation between buyer and seller (tenant and property owner). Free to work independently, employ real estate agents or other brokers or work within a larger brokerage firm, brokers are licensed professionals. While the requirements vary by state, broker licensing requirements include work experience (up to three years minimum), 60–90 hours of approved instruction and successful completion of a broker exam.

Brokers earn commissions—a portion of the transactions they manage. The listing agreement, a contract between the property owner and the listing broker, specifies the commission rate (6% is the norm but the rate is negotiable). Like residential real estate, the buying broker and the listing/selling broker split the commission.

Is it possible to save the buyer broker fee and simply conduct the transaction directly?

We wouldn't advise it.

Brokers work in the market every day and are likely to have an extensive network of contacts and local knowledge (information about sellers and properties that's not written down anywhere). Buying brokers will have an intimate knowledge of local tax laws, zoning regulations and access to crucial research (traffic patterns, demographic trends, business performance and property desirability). Buyer brokers analyze lease payment trends and requirements depending on the type of lease (single net, double-net, triple-net, or gross, see key terms later in this chapter).

Caveat emptor!

Let the real estate buyer beware.

Despite the clear value proposition, broker interests may not always align with the buyers they represent. Prioritizing personal income over the needs of the buyer, a broker might only show you properties with higher commission rates, advise you to pay a higher rent than necessary or push to close the deal sooner than is in your interests. Because commissions are negotiable, buyers can negotiate a flat fee.

Once again, like residential real estate, seller brokers represent the interests of the property owners. Unlike residential real estate it is common for seller brokers to play two roles. Serving first as the property owner's sales agent, these brokers may also serve as your property manager, which may affect your approach to negotiations, and you need to develop a working relationship with the broker.

PROPERTY MANAGER

Working on behalf of the property owner, a commercial property manager oversees and directs operations including maintenance of common areas (i.e., lawn care, snow removal and building repairs). Property managers also manage occupancy, address tenant needs and ensure lease compliance. Because occupancy is key to profitability of any commercial property, it is common for a seller broker to also serve as property manager for one or more properties.

LANDLORD (PROPERTY OWNER)

Owners of commercial property may or may not participate in the day-to-day operations of the properties they own. Property owners may not be a single person but a holding or development company that invests in a portfolio of properties and hires specialists (like seller brokers and management companies) to conduct ongoing business activities. Property owners negotiate your initial lease (and any lease renewals) and collect the lease payments and fees defined in your lease agreement, but that's not the extent of their role or responsibilities. Owners are responsible for ensuring compliance with building codes and managing foreseeable risks like water damage, equipment failures, security and structural integrity (roofing, electrical and heating, smoke and fire alarms) and may (depending on your lease terms) be responsible for certain maintenance and repairs.

Property owner or property manager effectiveness is important to you for several reasons. A property's appearance is a reflection on your business. How a property looks and perceptions of safety will affect the number and type of customers you'll attract. As most commercial properties are multi-tenant, the look and feel of the property will also affect the quality of businesses willing to occupy the property with you.

As you expand your business, you'll interact with different kinds of property owners, owner organizations, managers or management groups. It is common for a multi-unit franchisee to have leases with both large multi-state property owners and local people who own one or two centers. There are pros and cons to each, but the local owner is often more responsive and flexible than large holdings.

Difficulties working with multi-state property owners are often systemic, meaning that the system and not the people are the cause. Multi-state operations are larger and must manage the needs of many tenants across a wide geographic area. From a practical perspective, a single tenant among hundreds or thousands of tenants in a multi-state property system isn't as significant as being one of five or six tenants in a small strip mall. It is our experience that multi-state property owners tend to manage tenant relationships by-the-book.

Local property owners may only have one or two properties and a dozen tenants to deal with, so making individual decisions is less of a burden. However, the quality of property management, maintenance and the ability to attract premium co-tenant brands can vary widely among small property owners.

KEY TERMS & CONCEPTS

Knowing the players will help find the ideal site for your new business and negotiate lease terms that will position your new business for success. From your franchise real estate representative to your buyer broker, to your developing network of local market experts, you'll have people to help guide you through the lease negotiations. Having a basic understanding of terms used in the process helps you ask the right questions and lead the process.

LETTER OF INTENT

Moving from site search to commercial real estate negotiation begins with a Letter of Intent (or LOI) to alert the property owner of your formal interest in the property. The LOI includes a description of your business (what you plan to use the property for) and broadly defines the terms you desire. A starting point for negotiation, an LOI is a precursor to a formal agreement, and so does not include many of the details that will be in the lease.

Seek professional advice and work with your franchise representative before you submit an LOI. Don't offer an LOI until you are set on a site and ready to negotiate terms. Be respectful in your approach. It is not advisable to low ball (make an offer that's significantly below the listing price or current market range) if you really want the space. Anchoring your offer to the lower end of the current price range for similar properties isn't likely to offend—but every case is different, so seek the advice of experts in your market and from your ZOR. Remember, the selling broker or property owner can leave the table at any time if they feel you are not proposing serious terms.

THE LEASE

A commercial real estate lease is a type of contract, that defines what a tenant (leasee) of a property will pay the owner (lessor) of the property for use of that property. The legal owner of a commercial property grants certain use rights (i.e., occupancy) to the leasee in exchange for sum payment or payments. The lease sets out in writing the contractual obligations that will govern the lessor-leasee relationship. Leasing property is not the same thing as renting a house or apartment. Commercial leases are longer-term operational and financial commitments. Seek professional legal advice before entering into any agreement and take time to familiarize yourself with some of the more common lease terms.

TYPES OF COMMERCIAL REAL ESTATE LEASES

Complicated and often running counter to residential leasing experience, commercial real estate leases differ from straight forward residential leases that include all costs except for utilities. The fee for using the physical space (your rent) is simply one component of a financial formula that may include property taxes, insurance and common area maintenance.

There are four types of commercial real estate leases. Each type broadly reflects the distribution of certain financial expenses.

SINGLE NET

Single net leases require tenants pay property taxes.

DOUBLE-NET (NN)

The double-net lease requires tenants pay property taxes and insurance.

TRIPLE-NET (NNN)

The triple-net or net-net-net lease requires tenants pay property taxes, insurance and maintenance costs. One of the net expenses billed to tenants in a commercial triple-net lease, Common Area Maintenance (CAM) charges may vary over time and among geographies. For example, if you live in a snowy part of the country, your CAM fees may result from the frequency or cost of the prior year's snow removals or even a forecast for the coming winter. Not all leases include CAM charges, but some CAM fee structures can amount to 20% or more of the total lease expense. If CAM charges are a feature of your lease, make sure you thoroughly understand CAM calculations, when they are due and what protections you'll have from unexpected increases.

GROSS

Gross leases redistribute the expenses otherwise covered by the tenant in a single, double or triple net lease into a higher monthly rent. A gross lease may seem more desirable, but these costs don't disappear. A gross lease may seem more familiar (feels like a residential lease) and desirable as the property owner takes responsibility for property taxes, insurance and maintenance, but you can be sure that the increased monthly rent will be more than enough to offset the owner's additional cost.

TRADE OFFS

Each type of lease represents a tradeoff. While gross lease agreements offer a higher monthly rent in exchange for a single monthly lump sum payment, the amount of that payment may still vary significantly from year to year. Gross leases often include provisions allowing property owners to pass on increased expenses in the form of increased monthly rent. Depending on cashflow, direct payment of taxes, insurance premiums and CAM costs could help. If you are a seasonal business with an uneven cashflow, receiving a disproportionate percentage of revenues at one time, paying big ticket items while your business is cash rich and lowering your monthly cost for the rest of the year when cash is scarce may benefit you.

LEASE TERM

Generally considered the length of the lease, terms are either fixed, periodic or indefinite. Fixed leases end when the lease period ends. Periodic lease terms renew automatically at a specified interval (i.e., month, year). Less common, indefinite terms last for as long as both parties desire.

Fixed terms of five–ten years are common but something you should think deeply about. Years go by quickly and you really don't want to be moving locations every five years, but is ten years too long? Whatever you and your advisors decide, we'd also suggest investigating the inclusion of an option to extend the lease for two additional five-year periods after the initial term expires.

If options only benefitted the tenant, why would property owners ever consider including lease options? Typically, exercising an option extends the lease term and triggers a rate increase. So, if you want to keep a profitable unit going—no problem, it will just cost you a little more. For struggling units, you are still free to walk away. Without an option, the end of the term is just that—time to move on or start a new lease negotiation.

With or without options, if you are nearing the end of a term and you'd like to continue in the location, you'll need to develop a renegotiation strategy. Does the economic forecast look bleak? Does the center have one or more dark spaces (unoccupied units)? Is there new commercial real estate under development in the area? Circumstances like these, and others your franchise representative or buyer broker may suggest, provide powerful support for a lower renegotiated lease rate. The property owner may agree to lower terms but require that you sign a completely new lease, which may give you an opportunity to negotiate new end of lease options at rates lower than the original lease.

So complicated?

Seem like a lot of back and forth?

Welcome to the dance—the give and take of commercial real estate.

ACTIVITY: THE PARKING LOT CHALLENGE

As you progress in this book, we'll begin challenging you to "live" the franchise experience, to understand the roles and motivations of the people you'll be working with and to gain a direct and personal appreciation of the data and information you'll depend on to make important decisions. How can you prepare to make sense of a mass of market data or match location attributes to real space availability?

Multi-tenant shopping centers and malls provide one-stop convenience for shoppers, while smaller businesses enjoy access to larger numbers of customers than they'd generate alone. Depending on the type of franchise you are considering, your business may be the main traffic generator, or anchor, for the center. However, it is more likely that your franchise operation would benefit from locating in the same center as a big box retailer or other high-traffic anchors. Understanding the benefits of multi-tenant locations and the power of the anchor's draw are central to selecting the best site for your franchise business.

Driving the market and taking the parking lot challenge will help you develop an understanding of market dynamics, provide first-hand experience collecting traffic data and help evaluate shopping patterns. These experiences will prepare you for interacting with real estate experts and give you a better understanding of how to consume professional market research.

For this activity, you'll simply need to complete the following process and note your responses to the items containing questions. Do this for each property you are considering:

1. Explore the streets leading to and from the major shopping areas in your area.
2. Repeat the drive on different days of the week and weekends.
3. Which streets are busiest?
4. Was the traffic heavier in one direction in the morning and the other direction after work?

5. How might these traffic patterns affect your future business?
6. Do the sites you see match your franchisor's guidance for successful locations?
7. Once you identify the most promising areas, stop driving and park your car.
8. Find a quiet spot in a parking area, near a potential location.
9. Look around and observe shopping patterns.
10. Count the number of cars that come into the parking lot in one hour.
11. Repeat your one-hour count on at least two different days at different hours of the day.
12. Were the counts the same or did they differ?
13. Do shoppers stop at one store and then leave, or do they go from store to store to shop?
14. Are there more shoppers in the morning, at lunch or after work?

SPOTLIGHT: THE FIREMAN, JOHN CHADIMA

Firefighters have a well-earned reputation for strength and bravery. Rushing into a burning home, rescuing people from overturned cars or saving Tabby from the highest tree branch, all while carrying 50 pounds of equipment on their backs—takes calories! This might be why firefighters also have a reputation for big appetites and great cooking. It's part of the community-first culture that drew John Chadima to the growing fast-food franchise, Firehouse Subs.

"It's a chain that was founded by two brothers and former firefighters, Chris Sorenson and Robin Sorensen. They encourage restaurant owners and personnel to develop relationships with the local firehouse and other public safety departments and support the Firehouse Subs Public Safety

Foundation," says John, who opened his first Firehouse Subs franchise in 2014.

"I really wanted to have my own business and started looking around. I liked the franchise model where you weren't completely on your own. I'd operate my own business and still have the backing of an experienced team," he says. After completing his initial research, John flew to Firehouse Subs headquarters for a *Day of Discovery*. "It wasn't just a dog and pony show, but a real chance for prospective franchisees to meet the CEO and other restaurant owners face-to-face. It was clear that they wanted it to be a good fit on both sides. It was clearly a family-run business and I felt like I was becoming part of a family," Chadima continues.

John also recalled admiring the brand's commitment to give back to the communities in which they operate and was impressed by how Firehouse Subs structures the franchise. "If you chose the right brand, which I did, it's really the best of both worlds. An ideal mix of comfort and independence. Comfort from knowing there's an entire franchise system behind you, and independence in the fact that it's still your business," he explains.

Success and setbacks marked John's early franchise experience. "When we first opened, we came close to standing room only, but that slowed down and now we are probably 300-400 square feet too big." Why the change? When Chadima leased his first store, the center he selected boasted of two anchor tenants, a popular grocery store and a women's clothing outlet. Within one year of John's opening, both anchors closed their doors, resulting in a big drop in traffic. When leasing a franchise site, the physical space is only a small part of its value. A site's proximity to other businesses (especially anchor tenants) is a big part of the site selection equation.

Unfortunately for John, his lease did not include an often-overlooked clause stipulating what happens if other businesses in the center go dark, or other unexpected events like street closures or road construction projects hinder business operations. "I appealed to the property owner, over and over, asking for a little rent relief, but he wouldn't have it. [Dark clauses] used to be common, but not so nowadays. So, fight for that dark clause because a location with good traffic is essential and you can never predict what will happen," advises John.

Most franchisees aren't afraid of hard work and will do what it takes to keep their businesses afloat, but unforeseen and uncontrollable circumstances sometimes occur. That's one of the many reasons it's so important to select a franchise system with the experience to help you think about the small details that drive the biggest decisions. "When we first started looking, our realtor was really pushing locations that the franchise kept denying and thank God they did!" says John. Turns out, the franchise saw warning signs Chadima didn't see and gave his business the best possible chance for success. "We all make mistakes in life and business. It's how you bounce back that matters," John advises. Today John continues to grow his business, a wiser, more thoughtful operator with a deep commitment to his customers, employees and the communities in which his businesses operate.

CHAPTER 7:
STAFFING AND TALENT ACQUISITION

M oving from theory to practice, staffing your business will mark a tipping point in your franchise journey. This chapter explores how to find, screen and hire your team. Because staffing requirements and regulations vary by industry, geography and any number of other factors, we've framed our staffing discussion in terms of a common franchise model—the retail storefront—which encompasses a wide variety of franchise options from fast food to home décor, from massage to nail care and everything in between.

AKERS OF ADVICE: NOW FIRING!

Staffing is a two-sided coin. On one side, few franchising experiences rival the excitement of looking someone in the eye and saying, "You're hired!" The flip side offers an equal and opposite experience: The gut-punch reality of letting someone go. Remembering both sides of the coin and carefully selecting the right people for your team isn't about your needs alone. Job candidates are making an investment in you, your business and your judgement. Are you trustworthy? Realistic? Smart?

Accepting an offer to work for your business comes with an opportunity cost—the cost of surrendering any opportunities they'd get working elsewhere. Employee success starts before the first interview, before you put the "Now Hiring" sign in the window.

New to staffing?

The experience will be different from what you imagine.

Been hiring people for years in a corporate role?

Paying people with your own money changes everything.

Hired people for your own business, but never ran a franchise or entered a new industry?

The experience won't be the same.

A franchise pro venturing out to expand your operation?

What worked in one location won't produce the same results in a multi-unit operation.

When it comes to staffing, there's a lot to think about and the formula for success changes as circumstances change. For reasons we'll explain later in this chapter (see The Delicate Dance: ZORs, ZEEs & EEs), don't expect much in the way of staffing support from your ZOR. Instead, think through the fundamentals and take it one step at a time.

Whatever you do, don't put out your "Now Hiring" sign or start running

"Help Wanted" ads until you have a thorough understanding of the staffing requirements for your franchise model. Without intimate knowledge of your staffing needs, you'll run the risk of ending up with too many or too few employees, or even hiring the wrong kind of employees entirely.

No one single source or employment service is enough to support all your recruiting all the time, so get to know your options. Today's perfect marketing mix won't stay perfect for long. We live in a high-tech, media-rich environment, which continually produces new ways of engaging potential employees. Take time to stay current on what's out there—even if you are a franchisee superstar with a keen sense for hiring great people. Staffing problems will occur, and when they do they should not be ignored. Likely to grow, spread and become more serious, staffing issues rarely resolve themselves. That good feeling you get inside when you tell someone they're hired can fade quickly. Instead of a career opportunity, you'll be offering confusion and frustration—the key ingredients to employee dissatisfaction and separation. Without the knowledge and skill necessary to build your staff, a sign that reads "Soon Firing" would be more accurate. Finding the right mix (i.e., social media, referrals, employment agencies) to help you staff your business will come from many sources, not just this book. When these pages don't hold the answer, you need to remember the E (expertise) in TEMPO and reach out to others that have the expertise you don't.

THE BIG IDEA: STAFFING LOGIC

What does it take to operate your franchise model? Do you need 15 people or 50? Will everyone perform the same tasks at the same time? Or different tasks? At different times? Do some employees need special skills? And will everyone on the staff report to you or will there be a hierarchy?

There's a great deal to consider. That's why Jerry is often heard telling new franchisees to, "Slow your roll until you know the roles," and that's exactly where we suggest you start your process.

ROLES

Once again, we'll focus on a retail franchise operation, but the principles apply to any business. While your franchisor may not provide direct advice or support for your hiring process, your operations manual will include descriptions of the roles necessary to run your franchise model. If your manual does not include detailed role descriptions, you'll need to create them yourself. Role descriptions clarify the responsibilities and expectations of various staff members.

Role descriptions include the title of the role (i.e., General Manager, Manager, Assistant Manager, or functional staff like, cooks, delivery drivers, hairdressers, etc.) and a detailed description of the responsibilities of the role. Role descriptions define responsibilities and expectations for every position and indicate the wage (or wage range) you are willing to pay for each one.

What does a General Manager do differently than an Assistant Manager?

Are cooks excepted to occasionally cover the front counter?

How does one role relate to others?

Do cooks report to Assistant Managers, Managers or General Managers?

Let's say you operate a multi-unit franchise. Creating a General Manager position, a dedicated staff member to coordinate daily activities among your operating units makes sense. In fact, we strongly advise that you consider playing the General Manager role yourself, at least initially. Why? Assuming the franchise system you select is well-established, you'll participate in an extensive training program. You'll learn all the basics of running your business from the people that know the business best. However, nothing provides a better franchise education than showing up and engaging in the frontline operation of your business. Taking on a management role yourself will accelerate your learning and save cash in the early days when the business needs it the most.

SCHEDULING

Once you've found written descriptions of each role provided by your ZOR (typically found in your franchise operations manual) or you've written your own, you'll then determine the number of people you'll need to hire for each role. Once again, your franchise manual and other training materials are likely to provide scheduling guidance. If not, simply think through your operational needs step-by-step:

1. What is the minimum number of employees necessary to operate the business at any one time?

2. Will the business operate seven days a week, 24 hours a day, Monday through Friday 8 A.M. to 5 P.M., or another schedule entirely? Like many aspects of the franchise operation, the choice may not be yours to make. For retail franchise models, hours of operation are defined in your franchise agreement. While the

business is yours, customers don't think about each franchise unit as a separate business. They see a single brand and expect similar experiences, quality, pricing and availability wherever they go. That's why ZORs almost always mandate hours of operation.

3. During your hours of operation, will your business experience predictable peaks, periods where you'll likely see more customers than usual? For instance, a food service business may experience higher customer traffic around mealtimes and more traffic on the weekends than during the week.

4. What are your staffing needs when the business isn't open to the public? Bakers often bake the day's fare early in the morning, long before the doors open. Inventory, stocking and reordering are often tasks conducted during off hours and may not be done every day.

Armed with answers to these questions, you'll have all the information you need to develop staffing models and, when you are ready, begin hiring staff—a task that often demands more time and energy than new franchisees imagine.

SOURCING, RECRUITING & THE MARKETING MIX

Building your staff is not a onetime activity. Employee churn, particularly in service industries, is normal and expected which means that sourcing and recruiting talent will be an ongoing activity. Understanding this fact early on and taking the time to develop an active and continuous approach will serve you well.

The first question is how are you going to get the message out that you are hiring? Getting the word out about the positions you're looking to fill is the same as promoting your business to customers. You need to advertise! When you think about advertising, your mind may turn to thoughts of traditional media like newspapers, radio, TV and billboards. And while you may decide to use one or more of these outlets, it's likely your efforts will include healthy doses of digital and social media, job boards, placement services and simple word of mouth.

How do you develop a media plan that will provide a continuous flow of qualified candidates? The answer is different for every business, market and owner. For example, the messaging and marketing mix used to effectively attract candidates to a closet design company differs from those used to entice potential employees to work for a video game outlet. The perfect mix for a fast-food restaurant in Toronto may miss the mark in Phoenix. Promotional messaging reflects the personality and approach of the owner. Are you looking to create a team-based organization populated by self-motivated, self-directed employees or a top-down hierarchy that maximizes efficiency?

As you build your staffing promotion plan, you'll be evaluating many different types of media, some you know well, others may be new to you, and a few you might not have considered at all. We've put together a short list of media options worthy of your consideration and purposely excluded media that doesn't lend itself to employment advertising (like direct mail). And we've included one option that some might not classify as media—the employment party, which we've included because of the great results we've achieved with it over the years.

NEWSPAPERS & BROADCAST MEDIA

In a world gone digital, newspapers and broadcast (television and radio) are no longer the dominant local media choices. While newspapers and broadcast remain viable options, people (especially younger people) no longer look to newspapers or watch network television as primary sources of information. Rapidly declining circulation and viewership combined with a pricing model that charges for the delivery of targeted messages to an untargeted audience, suggest why newspapers and broadcast continue to lose ground among a growing number of efficient, highly targeted alternatives.

Big city newspapers, TV networks and radio stations that cover extensive geographic areas like Los Angeles, Houston or New York, make advertising cost prohibitive for many small businesses. Advertising in these markets means you'll be paying to send your message to jobseekers that may be too far away geographically to ever consider your listing. In smaller communities, the daily newspapers, local and cable television, and hometown radio stations may still be worthwhile. In fact, you might consider combining your employment advertising with your customer ads to increase your buying power and bring down the cost of both.

BILLBOARDS

Highly visible, productive and often expensive, outdoor advertising holds a unique place in the marketing mix. Billboards offer a great way to reinforce your messaging and improve customer recall when used in concert with other advertising outlets. Outdoor ads are less effective if used in isolation.

While there are many variations, there are three broad categories of billboards: static, digital and mobile. Static (or traditional) billboards display one message in one location for a period of weeks or months. You, the advertiser, pay for the design, production and installation of a giant canvas (or other material), which is affixed to a physical board. This means only one message can appear on a board at a time. Posting a new message takes a good deal of time and labor, so billboard companies generally require that advertisers rent multiple boards for many weeks or months. When using outdoor advertising to promote your ongoing business to customers, requiring multiple billboards over an extended period may work out nicely but the math doesn't work as well to attract a specific group of employees.

Digital billboards make outdoor much more attractive to franchise advertisers because digital message creation takes a fraction of the time and physical installation is eliminated. Digital displays also allow for message rotation, which means several advertisers can share billboard time on a single board or rent fractions of time on boards in many locations. Billboard owners generally require a minimum commitment of three to six months but may be flexible in allowing you to change out messages— switching from hiring employees to advertising your grand opening or special offer, all on one contract.

SOCIAL MEDIA

Social media has become the top choice for younger jobseekers. It's likely you'll experience the same thing in your business, so it is wise to consider all your social media options. As of the publication of this book, Facebook reigns and Twitter has given way to Instagram, so be aware that the social media landscape changes quickly. Difficulty managing a virtual environment that's always changing has spurred development companies that specialize in social media messaging. Virtual employment agencies like ZipRecruiter, Glassdoor, Indeed, Monster Jobs, LinkedIn and others offer a range of staffing support. While plans vary, the cost of finding a great candidate may be higher than you imagined. After all, you are offering someone a career, a paycheck and certain benefits, you'd think people would appreciate the opportunity you've created—and they do! However, virtual employment services are in the business of matching employees with employers, and they expect to be compensated for their efforts. While it's normal to experience a little employee acquisition sticker shock, consider the value high quality employees bring to the table. Use of an employment service is TEMPO-smart, getting you the expertise you need to hire the best possible candidates, reducing the stress that comes from the staffing process and freeing you to focus on other issues as you move closer to Opening Day.

VOCATIONAL SCHOOLS, COLLEGES & UNIVERSITIES

Many franchise models require specialized training, certification and/or licensing. Vocational, trade and technical schools and community colleges may offer training programs to teach the skills your business needs. These institutions are great places to search for candidates with the right skills. Thinking like a TEMPO-setter, you'll want to build a relationship with the institution so they know who you are and what you are trying to accomplish. To make those connections, you may want to sponsor events, offer to speak at career seminars or participate in an on-the-job training program where students earn class credit while working in your business. If your business requires specialized skills, certification or licensing, these institutions are especially important because they offer your business a continuous supply of the talent you'll need.

Does your franchise model require certified or licensed staff? The answer varies from state to state. While becoming an accountant, chiropractor, cosmetologist, hairstylist or lawyer requires specialized training almost everywhere, there are many other occupations that require some form of licensing as well, including: make-up artist (36 states), security guard (37 states), auctioneer (33 states), residential painting contractor (10 states), interior designer (4 states) and travel agent (8 states).

Other, less prescriptive forms of training may be every bit as vital to your success. Great candidates may be working through a management degree or certification program at a community college or university that requires on-the-job training experience. Posting opportunities with college career centers and bulletin boards or posting flyers in gathering places remain productive practices.

FAMILY, FRIENDS & THE COMPETITION

Being the TEMPO-setter you are, be ready to always share your story with others and include your need for new talent. As the number of family and friends who know your story grows, the number of people engaged in your scouting process increases too. The more specific you are about your needs, the more helpful they will be in identifying potential candidates. Don't hesitate to be direct. Ask them to think about someone who is looking for a job or perhaps who is underemployed (employed in a job that is well below their skill level).

Whatever product or service you'll be selling in your new business, customers are typically buying those products or services somewhere else right now. If you are opening a restaurant, your future customers are likely eating at other restaurants today, and of course you'd like these customers to frequent your establishment when it opens. That's the nature of competition. But what about the people that work for the competition? Are they off limits?

Poaching or trying to lure away a competitor's otherwise happy employees isn't something we recommend or encourage. There are ethical questions you'll need to answer to fit your values. That said, we do recommend that you experience the competition firsthand. Be mindful of the interactions with servers. Be on the lookout for people who fit your service standard and tell them how impressed you are with their performance. Ask them if they know anyone who's as good as they are that's looking for work. Give them a few of your business cards to offer other quality candidates and ask them to reach out if they ever want to change jobs. It's a fine line and it will be up to you how far you want to go to build your staff—always remember that if you do it now, it can be done to you later. And of course, be prepared for that one loyal employee to give your card to her boss and tell them you offered her a job. The worst that can happen is you get a call or two from concerned bosses. Simply let them know you were not trying to steal their staff employees, rather tell them about your new business in case someone they know is looking for a new job. In service and retail environments, staff move regularly until they find a forever-home. Many managers and owners recognize that most employees are open to better opportunities.

EMPLOYMENT PARTIES

Everybody loves a party! Build buzz and intrigue as you plan a night where people open to learning more about your employment opportunities can join you and your staff for a party. Like any other party, there are three essentials for success:

1. Food—Brings people together and gives you common ground to stimulate conversations that can help identify where they might fit in. Just showing up is a signal that they might see themselves as part of your team.

2. Gift bags—Small bags with inexpensive gifts, promotional items and coupons for your products or services. If they aren't going to be a member of the team, they might as well be a customer! To offset costs, seek supplier donations. Include coupons from neighboring businesses. Having the employment party conversation with

your new neighbors is often the start of co-marketing or strategic relationships.

3. Major prize drawing—Everybody loves to be a winner! Larger prizes stimulate more interest and more traction.

If the idea of employment parties is new to you, it's worth serious consideration. Intimidating to some—especially younger people who lack the confidence and experience to put their best foot forward in highly formal environments—the traditional process of screening candidates isn't the only way to evaluate talent. Observing potential candidates in a relaxed, social situation is a reasonable indicator of how they'll interact with customers and coworkers.

MESSAGING

Advertising is a many-for-few exercise. An advertiser pays a media outlet to deliver a message to an audience, only a fraction of whom will have an interest in the message. As a TEMPO-setter, you are always looking for ways to get more from every one of your advertising dollars. Crafting employment messages that not only pique the interest of potential candidates, but also introduce the brand to would-be customers is a TEMPO-setter best practice. After all, the reason you are advertising for a new staff is because you are opening a new business, right? Ensuring that your help wanted message informs the market that a great new business is opening soon is a good way to simultaneously build staff and interest in your new enterprise.

THE DELICATE DANCE: ZORS, ZEES & EES

From sales, marketing and operations to vendor management, information technology and real estate—franchise training exposes ZEEs to the various functions necessary to run their business. Not realizing the full extent of what's necessary to build sales, conduct an effective marketing campaign, rev up operations, engage vendors and get the right real estate for the right price, overwhelmed ZEEs can breathe a sigh of relief when their ZOR explains the resources the franchise system offers to make their job much easier. From social media tools to advertising assets, great franchise organizations surround franchisees with the help and support they need to run every facet of the business – except one.

ZORs won't be as prescriptive about employment as other aspects of the business. In fact, it is more accurate to say that your ZOR can't be as prescriptive and engaged with who you hire as they'd like. Sensitive and controversial, ZORs walk a fine line between providing best practice advice and avoiding operational mandate. If a ZOR mandates employment and training processes, the franchise system runs the risk of becoming the de facto employer and could assume employer liability—not a position any franchisor wants to be in. The situation reflects a longstanding debate regarding the relationship between the franchise organization and franchisee employee (EE).

The point of contention is this. If a ZOR sets out employment criteria, tells ZEEs how much to pay for each role, dictates every detail of every job description or even searches and hires employees on behalf of ZEEs, at what point do EEs really work for the franchise system and not the individual franchisee? For decades, the National Labor Relations Board viewed the ZOR's role as advisory (providing only basic guidelines to support the hiring process) and ZEEs as the employers of record. A few years ago, the National Labor Relations Board began to change its view of the franchisor–franchisee employment relationship, suggesting that certain types of support crossed the threshold from employment advice to employee control. At first glance you may think this is a distinction without much difference, but the ramifications are significant and far-reaching—not the least of which is the massive liability that would be thrust onto ZORs if the EEs from the entire system were suddenly considered corporate employees. Such an outcome is unthinkable to ZORs. The complexity, compliance requirements and the sheer size of the potential liability mean that ZORs generally temper the support services and advice they provide.

ACTIVITY: BUILDING YOUR ADVERTISING INVESTMENT SCHEDULE

In this activity, you'll create a spreadsheet to organize your media options. You'll apply your selections into a ranked list to help you formulate the right media mix.

1. Set your media budget for recruiting. Whenever you engage in media planning, either for recruitment or customer promotion, determine the amount of investment you're willing to make before you begin identifying media options. Why? Media budgets have a way of ballooning as new advertisers learn the power of mixing media to create results a small business can't achieve any other way. The trick is to learn what your media dollar can buy, while staying within your means. For this exercise, let's say your budget is $5,000 to hire your entire staff.

2. Label the first eight column headers: Outlet, Type, Circulation, Cost, Rank, Quantity, Total and Notes:

    a. Outlet—The name of the media company or publication, like the *New York Times.*

    b. Type—The category of media, like newspaper, radio, television, billboards, digital, etc.

    c. Circulation—The number of readers, viewers, listeners or sub-scribers who will receive your message.

    d. Cost—A rough estimate of the minimum investment necessary for you to utilize that form of media. For instance, it may cost you $100 to run a small help wanted ad but the newspaper sells space for ads that only run once. But you may need to run the ad twice a week for at least three weeks. Given this criterion, you'd enter an estimated cost of $600 ($100 × 2 times per week × 3 weeks).

    e. Rank—Leave this cell blank until you've completed the first draft of your list.

    f. Quantity—There are as many ways to package and purchase media as there are media types. Occasionally, the media purchase option will be expressed in units. For example, you may learn that the ad you want to run in the paper costs a certain amount each time it runs. Quantity allows you to test varying proportions of media mixes.

    g. Total—This is the sum of the proportional cost of each media option. Let's say the social media option requires a one-time fee of $2,000, then the quantity would be one and the total $2,000. Newspaper want ads might cost $300 each time you run the ad. If you think you'll need to run the ad ten times to get the response you need, that's $300 per ad run ten times for a total cost of $3,000.

3. Populate your spreadsheet with as many media options as possible. You may not have all the information you need to enter data into each column but that's okay, just document the information you do have. Now it's time to pick up the phone and contact the media outlets to secure a cost estimate and any other details you can. How many items should you have? We suggest about a dozen. It's likely one or two companies control billboards and mobile outdoor in your market, and the same is true for print. You'll have several television and cable options, many radio stations and an ever-increasing number of social media options to choose from.

4. Complete the first draft of your list by filling in the cost estimates for each option. If the media is sold for a single package price, consider that option as having a quantity of one. For media with a quantity, complete calculations by multiplying the quantity by the unit price. This should give you a total for each option in the total column.

5. With your initial cost estimates complete, count the number of options on your list. For this example, let's say your list includes 17 media options.

6. In the *Rank* column you've left blank up until now, it's time to order your options by ranking them from best to worst. For example, your best option is ranked number 1 all the way down to 17 (your worst option), if that's how many media types you're considering.

7. Sort your spreadsheet based on your Rank column so that the highest rank is at the top, then start a running total of the cost estimates for each option. With a budget of $5,000, if your #1 ranked choice costs $2,000—that's your running total. Because $2,000 is

less than your budget of $5,000, move to your next choices. Add on each amount until you've reached your budget total. Let's say your second and third choices cost $1,000 each. Your running total would be $4,000 ($2,000 for your first choice and $1,000 each for your second and third choices). The options listed fourth through eighth each have an estimated cost of $500. You'd add the fourth option, bringing your total to $4,500. Repeat the process until you've reached $5,000. In this case you'd stop after the fifth option, bringing your media plan in line with your budget. Of course you'll make lots of adjustments, but setting up your media options this way will help you understand your choices and guide your discussions with media reps.

We're purposefully keeping this initial draft simple. As you gain some experience using the tool, you'll want to add columns to your spreadsheet as you learn more about your options. For example, you may want to add contact information to create a single reference for all your media sales contacts.

This chapter is chock full of information, which can be a little overwhelming, so take your time and complete the media mix exercise. Not only will this activity help you make sound media choices to support your staffing needs, but the same process will help you organize your promotional media (see Chapter 8: Marketing, Promotion & You) as well.

SPOTLIGHT: THE MOM, CLARA OSTERHAGE

Working moms are inspiring, hardworking and savvy. Professional mothers must balance the demands of child rearing, careers and, time permitting, self-care. That's the story of Clara Osterhage—a story that reads like a novel about self-belief, hard work and perseverance.

"I was working in a hospital and had a bunch of people reporting to me, mostly nurses. I reported to a supervisor who kept giving me more and more responsibility," Clara recalls. She loved every minute of it—working with people and helping guide and direct their careers. Clara had two children at home and was expecting a third when she went on family leave. Returning a few months later, she discovered she'd been replaced! It hit her hard. Illegal by today's standards, Clara had no recourse at the time. She thought to herself, "What could be worse? That's when I was asked to train my replacement! Okay, I thought. That made it worse." As time passed, Osterhage began to feel restless and discontent—a common experience among mid-career workers with an entrepreneurial spirit who are open to new possibilities. That's when she saw an ad on TV about franchising—an infomercial featuring the hair styling franchise that would come to change her life.

Baby in tow, she ventured out to a local restaurant to meet with a franchise representative. "I made my decision on the spot and used my 403B (retirement account) and $75,000 I borrowed through the Small Business Administration to buy my first salon," she says. At the time Clara knew nothing about franchising, running a business or the beauty industry. Clara and her husband and business partner Ray were up and running in just two months, a head-spinning turnaround that is anything but normal. To make ends meet during the start-up phase, Clara had taken another job while managing the salon and raising three kids!

As candid as she is brilliant and determined, Clara confesses, "I had no idea what I was doing. At the time there was a shortage of stylists, so I got busy and sent out 766 letters—one to every stylist in the area." In the letter she introduced herself, described her vision for the new business and asked them to reach out to her. Within days she had scheduled 42 interviews and was on her way. After a stressful start, she thought her business was ready for a grand opening.

"It was a disaster! I was still working part-time at another job, and when I got off work I went to the salon and they were gone. They were all gone, the entire staff. Everyone walked out. I called Ray bawling and said, *'I think they all quit!'* Worst—day—EVER. But the silver lining was one stylist named Amy—my magical hire. Amy had worked for our biggest competitor in a store that was doing well, but she wanted to be a part of what we were going to build. Armed with my Magical Amy, a better benefits package and the upward mobility that comes from being in on the ground floor of a new enterprise, Amy and I recruited almost all of my competitor's staff. We never looked back."

Yet, questions remained. What had Osterhage done wrong? Why had her entire staff quit? How could she be sure it wouldn't happen again? "I realized I had not done a technical interview, and that's what sunk me," she says. The technical interview in the world of salons validates what each stylist can and cannot do. Simple questions like: Can you cut hair? Can you color hair? Clara had failed to ask these fundamental questions because she failed to follow the process set out by her ZOR—an error common among new franchise owners feeling the pressure to get the doors open. "I didn't even know the technical evaluation was a thing," says Clara.

With perseverance and motherly grit, she, Ray and Magical Amy were able to hang on and even grow during the early days. "We'd been operating for about a year and a half when we got a call from another franchisee. He had two stores and wasn't happy being a franchisee and wanted to sell. I told him I was interested but had no money. If we worked something out, he was going to have to be the bank. He agreed. Now we had three salons.

Look at us go! Not long after, my ZOR called to ask if I would take over another salon nearby and so, suddenly I had four stores!"

Using what she'd learned from hiring and supervising nurses, Osterhage quickly became an excellent HR leader. With four growing stores and a firm grasp on operational details, Clara finally quit her job as a recruiter and became a full time ZEE. Clara's gamble was starting to pay off, but to grow further she needed access to operating capital, a resource that's hard to come by if you have no track record running salons.

"We had to get very creative. As we grew, I had to have a line of credit should I need it. So after being turned down by several banks, I found a 20-something up-start banker who was trying to build the small business department," she says. His aggressive approach to giving small businesses the cash infusion they need, helped secure her first loan. More than that, she also found a partner and learned a critical lesson. Clara was a natural TEMPO-setter! Aligning her needs with a young banker looking to make a mark for himself taught her the importance of relationships. "That banker is still in my life. My secret sauce is relationships with key people. That is woven throughout our entire story. I've had the same attorney and accountant for years. They'd do anything for us," says Clara proudly.

Did Clara's big risk payoff in the end? We'll leave that up to you to decide. Today, Clara and Ray operate 73 stores in four states (mostly in Ohio) and have 720 employees. But that's not what makes Clara most proud. Her kids, one by one, are joining her in the business and making it a true family affair.

CHAPTER 8:
MARKETING, PROMOTION, & YOU

n this chapter you will learn the fundamentals of franchise marketing—
what to do and what to avoid. The chapter begins by explaining why
your operating agreement is likely to limit what you say, how you say
it and what you offer when promoting a business. We'll also explain why
it's in your best interest to adhere to your ZOR's policies. *Akers of Advice*
describes how to build and execute an effective marketing program. *The
Big Idea* examines how to measure marketing results and adjust your plan
on-the-fly.

AKERS OF ADVICE: LET'S GET REALLY SMALL

Stephen Hawking taught us that the secrets of the universe are found in
the *very large* and the *very small*. In other words, to understand the universe on a cosmic scale, you need to understand it on a subatomic scale.
While less dramatic, the formula for franchise success is no different. The
best brands didn't get that way by chance. Success is a combination of big
ideas and the little things you do or don't do, every day—the *very large* and
the *very small*.

Establishing a large-scale brand is incredibly difficult, but the hardest part
of building a great franchise system is striking a delicate balance between
brand consistency and local market flexibility. Superior franchise systems

clearly delineate what must be done the same way in every unit and what's best left to the ZEE's discretion, because no amount of brand savvy can account for local market nuance. Franchisors walk a fine line between control and support. The more operational control a ZOR exercises, the more legal responsibility the franchise system assumes:

- *Flexibility and control are inversely related—the more of one, the less of the other.*
- *Control and risk are positively correlated—the more of one, the more of the other.*

ZORs and ZEEs are business partners. The threats or weaknesses of the ZOR are the threats and weaknesses of the ZEE. When it comes to marketing, the challenge is to balance the requirements necessary to ensure local marketing activities uphold and strengthen the brand's image with the operational flexibility ZEEs need to address local market needs. While the marketing function does not present the same legal risks ZORs face when it comes to employment (see Chapter 7: The Delicate Dance)—ineffective, haphazard or poorly executed local marketing efforts can damage the brand and adversely affect other owner-operators.

Like the universe itself, the secrets of franchise excellence are found in the very large and the very small. Intrinsically connecting global brand operations with what you do on your block—adhering to marketing guidelines—will strengthen the system, while still maintaining your independence and creativity.

As you will learn, your ZOR has the very large (brand marketing) covered, so let's turn back the clock to 1977 and do what Steve Martin suggested on his album of the same name, Let's Get Small! Let's get really small with small-business marketing for franchise operators.

THE BIG IDEA: MARKETING VS. PROMOTION

At the dawn of the 20th century, U.S. retail magnate John Wanamaker put into words what far too many marketers experience when he said, "Half my advertising spend is wasted; the trouble is, I don't know which half." The quote has become cliché, a truism about how little we know about the effectiveness of our advertising and promotional investments.

In a world saturated with promotional messaging, from TV shows that are more commercial than entertainment to websites that sell instead of share, it's easy to feel like an expert. As a layperson, that's not an issue. As a franchise operator, believing you have a better understanding of marketing, advertising and promotion than you do, can be costly. Let's begin with a review of what marketing is and how it relates to the operation of a franchise business. We'll then examine the role of the promotional mix in building customer relationships.

THE MARKETING MIX

It is difficult to overstate the amount of time and effort it takes to determine a brand's optimal marketing mix. Unless, of course, you happen to be a franchisee in a great franchise system that's accumulated the marketing experience of hundreds (sometimes thousands) of system operators. They've lived it. As the conduit, the common thread that runs through the entire franchise system, ZORs are singularly positioned to drive portions of the marketing effort while looking to ZEEs to complete it.

The American Marketing Association defines marketing as, "the process of identifying customer needs and determining how best to meet those needs." If you have marketing experience or have taken classes on the subject, you may already be thinking about the marketing mix—the 4 Ps of marketing (price, product, place and promotion), which is the set of tools you'll use to meet the customer needs you've identified. Defining promotions gets a little trickier, as some concepts overlap and the distinctions become less clear. For purposes of this discussion, let's consider marketing (and the marketing mix) as customer strategy, and promotions (and the promotional mix) as the tactical plan to execute the marketing strategy.

The 4Ps of marketing not only build brands —they are powerful standardization tools.

PRICING ZORs generally set prices nationally with some variation for regional areas. Standardized pricing helps ensure that customer value is consistent across the system.

PRODUCT Standardization is a brand-building hallmark. For this reason, ZORs generally spare no effort to minimize or eliminate brand variances.

PLACE Relating to how products and services get to the customer, place includes distribution channels and intermediaries. . In Chapter 6: Selecting Your Site, we discussed some of the many real estate requirements ZORs deploy to ensure a uniform look and feel among operational units.

PROMOTION Dealing with all aspects of communicating marketing messages, ZORs and ZEEs each play key roles in promotional activities. ZORs provide the corporate image campaigns, brand messaging, collateral material templates, graphics and special promotions for the entire system. ZEEs use the promotional materials and messaging provided by corporate to support local media and marketing activities.

The franchise brand is the primary asset of any franchise system. Protecting the brand is job one, and that's why marketing support is one of the most valuable and important aspects of becoming a franchise operator. To illustrate the point, consider the following scenario in which one of the world's best franchises fails to use the 4Ps to support brand integrity.

Special note: This scenario is hypothetical and in no way a reflection of the approach or actions of the McDonald's Corporation and is used purely for illustrative purposes. We may be overly risk adverse, but we don't want any McLawyers knocking at our door.

MCWHATNOW?

Imagine you are traveling away from home in another state. You've had a hard day and you're missing home and out of the corner of your eye you see McDonald's, a comfortable brand that reminds you of home. You roll your rental car into the drive thru, do a quick scan of the menu kiosk, see that a Big Mac is $5.99 and place your order. Feeling a little better and back on the road, you notice another McDonald's a few blocks away—only this restaurant has a huge sign out front that reads, Big Mac Half-Price Sale. How would that make you feel? Saving $3 may not be a budget buster, but had you known that a better deal was only blocks away you might have waited a few minutes to get the lower price from the cheaper outlet. The scenario is worse for a cost-conscious family of four because the $3 difference becomes $12. The experience is a system killer. Pitting units of the same franchise system against one another counters the benefits of franchise system membership. Pricing is only one of many tools ZORs use to protect their brands and system operators. Product consistency is just as critical.

Rolling back our story to the drive thru. You've ordered a Big Mac, and at the pick-up window you received your sandwich. All good so far, but when you open the Big Mac box you don't find two all-beef patties, special sauce, lettuce, cheese, pickles, onions on a sesame seed bun. Instead, you see something that looks and smells like tuna fish sandwich on pita bread. Nothing against tuna fish or pita bread, but that is clearly not what you ordered. So, it's back to the drive thru to lodge a complaint. Surprisingly the manager tells you that each restaurant creates its own version of the Big Mac and suggests you'll love theirs if you just give it a try. How are you feeling now? Product and service consistency are franchise success imperatives—even if you like tuna fish better than burgers.

Rewind to when you first saw the McDonald's sign on the street. You pull into the parking lot and instead of the familiar drive thru, you follow a long path that leads into a dark alley. When you finally arrive, the restaurant doesn't look like any McDonald's you've ever seen. The golden arches are purple triangles, and the windows are blacked out. I'll bet that tuna-based Big Mac is looking pretty good right now. Physical plant consistency is a franchise success essential. The look and feel of the facility reassure customers that they are in the right place and will receive the products and services they have come to expect.

Mirroring the logic of price and place consistency, promotional standardization ensures that customers aren't forced to shop among franchise units to find the best deal. The price is the price and, while there may be some variation within a region or market, consistency is key. Just as customers find reassurance in physical plant consistency, the look and feel of promotional materials support brand integrity and are among the many reasons ZORs require the use of a standard set.

To be clear, McDonald's is one of the greatest franchise brands ever created.

The McDonald's brand maintains the highest level of brand integrity, and it is for this reason alone that we chose to use it to illustrate the importance of the 4Ps and why ZORs must enforce 4P consistency.

MARKETING FEES

As a member of your franchise system, you will be expected to contribute a percentage of your monthly gross sales receipts to help fund the marketing effort. The rate varies among ZORs, and ranges from the low to mid-single digits. These marketing funds are earmarked for system-wide promotions and events designed to build brand recognition and drive business. ZORs create standardized marketing materials and templates, handle national media and secure sponsorships that support the entire system. Your ZOR may also require that you contribute to a local or regional marketing co-op to support marketing activities in your area and spend a certain amount or percentage of your revenues on local promotional activities.

ZEEs often express disappointment about having to pay into these funds, until they learn that there's much more power and value in a collective marketing investment than could be generated by a single ZEE alone. How many small businesses (not franchises) in your town could afford to advertise in the Super Bowl, or sponsor a professional sports team or event and get the brand message out to hundreds of millions of people? Of course only a small portion of those viewers or attendees are potential customers, but there will be a percentage in that mix. It's not uncommon for someone to come up to one of us and say, "I saw that you sponsored the College Football Playoff Series," recalled one ZEE. ZORs leverage the collective contributions of the ZEEs, conduct research to select the right investments and manage the production process.

It is hard to part with a portion of every dollar for a marketing fund you don't control, especially when you are just starting out and you are not yet profitable. To help with the adjustment, learn everything you can about the process in your franchise and interact with the people who run the program. Don't be shy. It is your money and your business.

THE PROMOTIONAL MIX

If marketing fees take care of building brand awareness, national and regional advertising and the creation of marketing materials, what's left for the ZEE to do? Plenty! ZEEs transform the interest and awareness generated at the system level into customer trial, return visits and ultimately customer loyalty.

Are you wondering if you know enough about executing local promotions to get the best results?

Stop worrying.

You are part of a franchise system and won't be facing these problems on your own. No matter the issue, there's a very good possibility that another franchisee, or more likely many other franchisees, have faced the same challenge. Many ZORs also direct a portion of your marketing fees to fund staff dedicated to helping you develop and execute your promotional plans.

As the marketing mix defines the brand strategy (price, product, place and promotion), the promotional mix identifies the promotional options you've selected to achieve your objectives. Promotional options change with the times. Today's hot promotional vehicle may be old news tomorrow. Digital media marketing is an excellent example of a promotional vehicle that didn't exist a generation ago, but today is a staple of small business promotion.

Franchisees develop two promotional plans, internal and external. You'll develop the internal plan to help you attract the talent you need to staff your business (see Chapter 7: Staffing & Talent Acquisition). Your external plan will focus on customer trial, engagement and retention. These plans will likely include a unique blend of advertising, personal selling, local sponsorships, direct marketing, public relations, corporate image and product placement.

If ZORs are so adept at the marketing mix, why don't they handle the promotional mix as well? The answer is simple: customer traffic flow. Like the flow of vehicles on a highway, businesses experience customer traffic patterns. When things are good, your business will feel like a freeway at rush hour. Other times, it might feel more like a single-lane, dirt road that's populated by tumbleweeds. Industry, location, seasonality, time of day or week, brand reputation and any number of additional factors may influence the timing and severity of the peaks and valleys of your customer traffic pattern. You don't have to be an experienced franchisee to realize that your goal is to maximize high-traffic opportunities and minimize low-traffic periods.

Without careful planning, you may be caught off guard, overstaffed, understaffed or simply unable to respond to predictable customer traffic changes. An otherwise competent franchisee might end up unnecessarily tapping credit lines or spending rainy day resources, leaving the business vulnerable when the truly unexpected happens.

It's easy to see that a food franchise will see more traffic and sell more food during mealtimes. Sub-segments of the food franchise categories may experience variations of this pattern. An ice cream parlor would likely sell more ice cream in warm weather and experience higher traffic in the hours after traditional mealtimes. A food franchise operating in a resort town would have traffic patterns that mirror the seasonality of the visitors.

While overcoming customer traffic patterns isn't difficult, the solution is unique for each franchise location making it highly impractical for a ZOR to manage and execute the local promotional mixes. The role of the ZOR is scale, brand integrity and best practice operations and systems. The role of the ZEE is to tailor a promotional mix to fit the local community.

The number and types of promotional activities are continuously changing. Only a few years ago social media was untested, unproven and generally considered fringe or experimental. Today, social media sits firmly at the core of most retail franchise promotional efforts.

GUERRILLA MARKETING

In 1984, Jay Conrad Levinson coined the phrase Guerrilla Marketing to describe marketing efforts that use unexpected or unconventional inter-actions as a method of promotion. Levinson focused on ways to create direct contact with customers and deliver emotionally charged messages. The concept proved enduring. Four decades later, guerrilla marketing has become synonymous with any nontraditional approach to local market promotions.

Over the years, Jerry modernized the tactic by focusing on repeatable, low or no-cost, hyper-local activities proven to drive near real-time customer traffic. It's what he calls the Customers On Demand (COD) promotional mix. Designed to support local franchise health and promote growth, COD is all about giving small businesses a big presence in the neighborhoods where they operate. Or as Jerry puts it, "Visibility, visibility, visibility."

CHEATER SIGNS

Picture a real estate yard sign. Now make it a little smaller and very inexpensive. That's a cheater sign, and they should be part of every retail franchise operation. Typically made of plastic or plastic-coated cardboard and attached to a wire frame, cheater signs provide a cost-effective, reusable way to communicate a simple message. Imprinted with any slogan, price point, or configuration, including arrows directing traffic toward your front door, cheater signs are an ideal way to promote grand openings (see Chapter 9: Opening Day), special events and sales.

PLACEMENT

The wire frame that supports the message board extends out from the sign itself for a few feet, providing a simple and easy way to secure the sign into any soft ground. Placed anywhere from steps outside your front door to a mile away, well-placed cheater signs will attract the attention of people in close physical proximity to your location—potential customers that don't have to do much to satisfy an impulse to stop by your business. The job of the cheater sign is to create that impulse. It is important to place signs far enough away from your location to allow drivers to make a safe entry into your center.

SHORT PERIODS

Cheater signs help boost traffic for short periods. More signs are better than too few, but leaving cheater signs out for too long (more than a week or two) transforms the sign from timely message to eye sore. Used sparingly, cheater signs will drive customer traffic. As Jerry stated in his chapter introduction, when it comes to cheater signs, think small, really small. For example, if your business slows between 1 P.M and 4 P.M. weekdays, put out a few signs along the entryways just before 1 and take them down around 4.

SHOCKINGLY ATTRACTIVE OFFERS

Cheater signs will get the attention of potential customers, but that's all they can do. It's up to you to provide a compelling message or what Jerry calls "a shockingly attractive" offer. Of course, you'll have to work within the pricing guidelines of your franchise agreement, which may limit some of your options, but you can get creative with added value offers and give-aways. We suggest you think about new, first-time customer transactions as investments. You'll invest all of your profit on the initial transactions to secure new customer relationships and longer-term profits.

CLUSTERED MESSAGING

Cheater signs are small; too small to display entire sentences that can be read from a moving car. That's why the COD approach includes what Jerry calls clustering. He will break up a message into several signs, placed and spaced so that drivers are able to see the entire message as they pass by the cluster. This explains why Jerry's warehouse features an array of commonly used cheater signs that read SALE or FREE. He mixes and matches signs to create the message he needs for the moment.

Arrows are the most common sign in Jerry's inventory. Why? Because the most effective COD messages always include directional arrows.

THE LAW IS THE LAW

Public signage is regulated by local sign ordinances. Cheater signs may not be appreciated or welcomed by those that enforce the ordinances—people Jerry calls the Sign Police. The rules governing cheater signs vary among municipalities. In some cases, you may need a permit. In other cases, it may be a matter of how long your signs are displayed. Placing cheater signs to support a weekend sale, then removing the signs Sunday night may be all you need to avoid dealing with sign enforcement.

Always looking to adhere to the law, while still achieving his objective, Jerry even mounts cheater signs in car windows. Since cars are personal property, displaying a sign in the window of your parked vehicle is generally permissible.

One of our store managers completed training on cheater signs and their impact on store growth. She employed the cheater sign tactic and made a big impact on our annual marketing event.

Following the training, she mapped out a geographic sign sketch. She decided to go out a mile in every direction. She then identified businesses in those areas. Then the brilliant move—she negotiated with the owners or managers to park our employees' cars, complete with a windshield cheater sign, displayed in their lots to guide traffic toward our location.

Her plan worked so well that her unit set a customer traffic record that would not be broken for several years. This carefully executed tactic generated new clients who continue to come back for many years. All with the use of a $5 cheater sign!

Special note: Consult and read the sign ordinances for your municipality. These can be found in the planning and zoning section of the municipality's website. There will be lots of jargon, so look specifically at the sections relating to any of the tactics mentioned here that you plan to utilize.

There is nothing glamorous or pretty about these tasks. These are simply boots-on-the-ground concepts that drive customers into your establishment at a minimal cost. Using short-term and very specific time frames, they will absolutely drive customers-on-demand to your store.

SIGNS & BANNERS

Like cheater signs, signs and banners are a critical component of your guerrilla marketing toolkit. Unlike cheater signs, costs for signs and banners will be higher, will garner more attention and deliver a much more detailed message, but signs and banners require a temporary sign permit from the city and will be more time-consuming and difficult to install.

FLAGS

Flags come in all shapes and sizes, are colorful and they move. The most common of which are vertical 8–15 feet tall designs. You can even use a series of flags in a row to increase exposure and drive customer response. Easy to maintain and install, flags come with either a semi-permanent ground stake or a metal base and are often collapsible and easy to store when not in use.

LET YOUR FREAK FLAG FLY!

We We had just opened a new store in a municipality we had not dealt with before. We were rapidly approaching our annual sale and needed to deploy some guerrilla marketing tactics to really ramp up our sales.

Meeting with the building and zoning representative, it was clear that the city had absolutely no tolerance for our monkeying around with signs. Jerry pulled out the data card and shared a study that documented a 30% increase in sales in the periods immediately following our use of COD tactics. In a way that only Jerry could, he asked, "Are you telling me that the city is going to force my family and our staff to forego that economic development just to protect a sign ordinance?" Stunned, the bureaucrat candidly shared that no business owner had ever produced metrics like that before. As proof the impossible can happen, the Sign Police made an exception for the sale.

When the annual sale came around again, it was time for Jerry to approach the city once more. What he learned surprised and delighted him. The bureaucrat loved his approach so much, he took pictures of the presentation and used them to convince the city council to change the ordinance. The new rule granted permission for the use of flags during one-week timeframes, up to four times a year without approval and at no cost to the business owner.

WRAPPED VEHICLES

Ever seen a wrapped vehicle? You know those colorfully decorated vehicles advertising a business. If you're like us, you've probably seen one and said to yourself, "I would never drive that (fill in the blank...gaudy, ugly, embarrassing) car."

Having your life savings wrapped up in a business and your entire income dependent on that business, might increase your willingness to drive a wrapped vehicle. Whatever your preference, it's hard to argue with the reach and visibility of a wrapped vehicle as you drive it through town.

Jerry made the decision for his business to get a wrapped vehicle, when "I saw a city bus coming around the corner wrapped in an ad for our biggest competitor and thought 'How am I going to compete with that?' I pulled to the side of the road and called the city bus department to find out how they did it. They were gracious enough to offer me the opportunity to also advertise on their buses for a small fee of $12,000 a year. End of conversation. Too rich for my blood. Back in traffic, I then had to dodge a dangerous-looking black Volkswagen Beetle wrapped in an ad for a big box electronics store and thought I could afford one of those. Soon we were the proud owners of a fire-engine red Volkswagen Golf. Within days we were getting feedback from customers that they were now seeing us everywhere. Today we have a fleet of wrapped vehicles and trailers, which we use for public events like parades, and we park them in front of our stores as a portable billboard."

LOGO GEAR

Logo gear is one of the simplest, most enjoyable and possibly least expensive options to build brand awareness. If your business doesn't require specific attire, one of your first steps as a new business owner should be to have logo gear made. Conversations that began with a simple glance at our logo, often led to long-term relationships otherwise missed if not for a simple logoed shirt. Years later it is rewarding to see how a couple logoed shirts, pens, golf balls and other items helped us build our brand. Commonly referred to as swag, imprint items can be part of the shockingly attractive offers you feature on your cheater signs.

DIRECT MAIL

While direct mail may feel outdated, several studies report increased response rates that position direct mail third on the promotional mix pecking order behind only social media and email marketing.

Direct marketing is a way to communicate a commercial offer by speaking directly to potential customers. Also known as direct response marketing, the vehicle provides a wide range of mechanisms to solicit and process customer responses from coupons to 800-numbers, reply-cards and forms. Response rates refer to the number or percentage of customers that take an action based on seeing an advertisement and vary based on the type of promotional vehicles you employ but are often as low as one or two percent. It is not surprising if a direct mail campaign that distributes 10,000 coupons only yields one hundred or so walk-ins to buy your product or try your service.

Selecting the right mechanism has been shown to boost your response rates by 135%. Direct marketing is sent to pre-selected lists of potential customers typically based on geography (zip code), prior purchasing history or participation in other lists. The goal of direct marketing is simple: Sell directly to customers without all the middlemen. Direct mail has been popular for decades, topping 150 billion dollars in 2010. The biggest challenges are to properly source your mailing list and to make sure your message is delivered at the right time. Well-qualified lists can increase your response rate three times, while appropriately timed messages can double it.

Direct mail can be hit or miss. While traditional media (newspapers, radio and TV) differ dramatically from market to market, direct mail options are similar across markets, which means your ZOR should be able to provide valuable guidance as to what works and what to avoid.

COUPONS & FREEBIES

Long before the emergence of Big Data, Jerry was firmly in the camp of Small Spreadsheet. He tracked as much data as possible. Jerry's wife Mickey introduced an app that created barcodes to identify each event and offer. These barcodes were then entered into their point-of-sale system, so when a customer presented a coupon or flyer the barcode could be scanned and tracked. Understanding both your investments and their returns is a critical component to creating the optimal promotional mix.

SPOTLIGHT: THE C.H.O., MICKEY AKERS

My wife, Mickey, had cancer as a young child, an experience that forever magnified the importance of the work of non-profit and cause-related organizations. When we'd just started dating, Mickey and I attended an

American Cancer Society fundraiser and we've been committed to that organization ever since. Our daughters, Shelly Dorman and Sam Reges, share our passion by working on the Muscular Dystrophy Association telethon. At first, they checked in presenters and then graduated to training and managing phone volunteers. Over the years, we've also built relationships with The Boys and Girls Club, Veteran's Association and other great organizations.

We'd never connected the work of these organizations with the work of our franchise, but that all changed when we attended a family-friendly fundraiser that struggled to engage (wall-off, corral) the children in a way that allowed their parents to fully participate. Determined to always add value, we thought of ways to solve the problem and decided to focus on giving the kids an experience of their own.

Were we volunteering to be babysitters? Not a chance! We were thinking more about providing a little entertainment. Mickey and I had just bought our first franchises and we wanted to get our name out in the community. The idea was simple. Our associates would entertain the kids (think temporary tattoos, stickers and balloons—maybe even colored hairspray) and give out a few coupons.

The results were astounding. We got great feedback. And this simple gesture solved a real problem. Most importantly, the kids loved it. Of course we were able to give out several hundred coupons. And as we've discussed, a typical yield for direct mail can range between 1-4%. So you can imagine how delighted we were with a 20% redemption rate on our very first event. Not only did that number exceed our expectations, but many of the participants came in the very same day.

There is also a community-building aspect for our associates when staffing booths. A pride in ownership and the opportunity for them to work together outside the normal business environment made these events team-building exercises. And of course, whenever they need a little boost, we can always call in Mickey—our Chief Hugs Officer (C.H.O.).

CHAPTER 9:
OPENING DAY

T raffic patterns analyzed, site selected, terms negotiated, lease signed, architectural designs approved and general contractor buildout complete, it's time to bring your dream business to life. In this chapter you will learn how to plan, staff and execute your GO plan—the promotional campaign plan you'll use to support the grand (G) opening (O) of your new business. First, Jerry discusses why staffing your grand opening and training your new employees is your top priority. *The Big Idea* details why promotions, hiring, training and soft openings are critical to your GO! *Spotlight* features the story of how a daughter of two South American missionaries and a former corporate executive cooked up what is today a thriving bakery operation.

AKERS OF ADVICE: STAFFING THE OPENING

A few years ago, we opened a new unit, in a new market. We created what I call a GO plan, detailing the promotional activities used to support the event. Everything, except one thing, was on track—staffing. Because the new unit was far away from where we lived, we'd taken up residence at a nearby hotel and had meals at local eating establishments.

As opening day approached, our staff struggle intensified. At dinner we were lucky enough to be served by an amazing young woman. While it was clear that she was just starting her career and had a great deal to learn about customer service, she took great pride in the way she looked.

Over the course of our conversation, I mentioned my new business which was in the beauty industry. She talked about her career aspirations and prior experience, both of which aligned nicely with the type of personnel we were looking for. We scheduled an appointment for an interview the next day. Soon after we had our newest employee. It was clear she was much happier working in the industry she always aspired to be part of and working within an organization that appreciated both her skills and her pride in her work.

A few days later, Mickey and I ate at another restaurant, had a similar conversation with another server and filled the last open position. Being able to identify unexpected potential, wherever and whenever it shows, is a powerful franchisee skill. As a point of clarification, we don't generally engage with the staff of other local businesses with the intent of enticing them away—what we call in the business *poaching*.

Today sourcing and attracting talent require a plan all its own (See Chapter 7: Staffing & Talent Acquisition). The most successful GO plans employ multiple promotional tactics. You never know where your customers will hear about you. Often a new customer will hear about your business many times before they consider patronizing your business.

While constructing your GO plan starts as early as possible, executing your plan begins as your general contractor finishes the build-out, signage goes up, the point of sale system is installed and your business looks ready to welcome customers.

Not a single event (more like weeks, months or multiple months), grand openings are as complex as they are important, so ask for and accept help wherever you can find it. Your ZOR will provide planning and execution guidelines, and often supply sample plans or share successful plans used by other franchisees.

Make no mistake about it, your staff will determine the success of your enterprise. Your grand opening is a one-time opportunity, a chance to make a first impression with potential customers. And the results of your grand opening will impact your customer counts for years.

THE BIG IDEA: STAFFING YOUR GRAND OPENING

Clients don't care if hiring is tough, if there aren't enough applicants or if you can't get staff to show up to work. When you open the doors on your grand opening, you'll need a staff that can provide great service from the first customer to the last. Hiring and training staff for a GO is critical and often overlooked. While we discussed staffing and talent acquisition in Chapter 7, there are a few special considerations when it comes to staffing for your grand opening.

1. Approach hiring by starting at the top. Hire your key managers first as they need more training and time to become proficient in their roles. In addition, you'll want these key players to participate in the hiring process and the training of front-line workers.

2. The primary goal of a grand opening is to build a robust customer base and generate initial cash flow. To that end, you will need more employees during your grand opening than during normal operations.

3. Train new hires as soon as possible. It is important for every employee to understand how to deliver superior customer service. Do not abdicate this process to a new manager, until he or she consistently demonstrates the level of service you want replicated by your staff.

4. Because you are opening a new business, you won't have the opportunity to provide real-world training with customers, that happens after you open. Which is why our training program includes sending new hires to work in other locations, either ours or other ZEEs. Creating educational opportunities like these provides hands-on experience and accelerates the training process.

5. Not all staff will succeed. The business may not be the right fit for them. So don't get too emotionally involved in the process or you'll become frustrated.

6. Keep your eyes open for the diamonds in the rough among your new hires. These high-potential employees are the ones you'll want to identify, support and eventually train to grow with you.

In today's employment environment, applications don't have a very long shelf-life. It is likely the candidates applying to your business have applied to many others as well. Respond quickly, schedule an interview and—if they are a fit—hire them.

PROMOTIONAL OPPORTUNITIES

GO plans define the promotional vehicles you'll use to get the word out about your new business. GO plans include costing, so the plan must be reflective of the budget. The plan should be designed to hit a broad cross-section of your target market and be spread over a specific time frame to gradually educate and attract customers. Each franchise model and location will likely need different advertising vehicles to hit all the potential customers you want to attract. Below is a list of things to consider when putting together your GO plan, and to use for ongoing marketing as you grow and prosper.

1. The old standby—Television. Offering great visibility and coverage, TV is also very expensive. Typically, TV is used by ZORs as a part of their national marketing programs but could be used in support of a local grand opening if you are able to negotiate an affordable advertising schedule.

2. Radio—moderate expense, with great reach and offering the opportunity to target specific audiences, radio remains a viable promotional option for local businesses. Station format (news talk, sports, music) provides readymade audience segmentation. The downside is that you may need to advertise on multiple stations to reach your potential customer base.

3. Newspapers have long been an advertising staple. Today, younger generations tend to get their news and exposure to advertising elsewhere, as a result, newspapers have become a lot less relevant. Still print publications, like weekly mailers or inserts, are great distribution tools.

4. Billboards are a steady and reliable resource to build drive-by traffic counts and brand awareness in your area. While billboards can get

pricey (especially the digital boards), billboards remain one of the best most cost-effective promotional vehicles.

5. Guerrilla or COD marketing (see Chapter 8: Marketing, Promotion & You) is ideal for most retail, food and direct service businesses. It is inexpensive, simple to implement, and it can be turned on and off with little to no notice. Cheater signs, banners, wrapped vehicles, sign wavers or mascots and community events may be the most effective and lowest cost-per-customer acquisition approaches you can use.

6. Digital Marketing—exploding in recent years, online and social media marketing have become the make-or-break promotional vehicle for the modern ZEE.

Over the years countless ZEEs, bubbling with enthusiasm, have approached me with the build-it-and-they-will-come mindset. These new business operators recount conversations in which people indicate that they've been waiting for their new business and will buy, use, visit all the time. While encouraging, these comments most often lead to a false sense of security, convincing new ZEEs that they need not execute a complete GO plan because their business is destined for greatness. While I'm not the type to dampen anyone's excitement, I caution them not to let these individual perceptions minimize the priority or investment they make in their grand opening.

SOFT OPENING

Think of a soft opening as a dress rehearsal. It is an opportunity to perform for a crowd of interested people for a few hours before it all counts. To develop your own soft opening, simply pick a date a few days before your formal grand opening. Invite family, friends and neighbors to try out your product or service and direct your team to handle the soft opening, just as they would any normal day providing great service to your guests. The benefits of a soft opening far outweigh the costs.

Soft opening benefits include:

1. An opportunity to practice customer service with a kinder, gentler audience that is there to support your new business.

2. Real-world experience—soft openings are a great middle ground, allowing you to find gaps in performance that you remediate before it's for real.

3. Your staff will quickly gain confidence in their ability to deliver great customer service. In fact, it's likely you'll see a gradual improvement in performance throughout the soft opening.

4. Generating a buzz, attracting attention from neighbors and others curious about your new business.

5. An opportunity to generate word-of-mouth advertising when people turn up uninvited. Let them stay and build new relationships and foster goodwill in the community. You might say, "Today is only a practice run with a select group of people. Since you're here, we'd like you to be part of that group. Please come in, try our product or service and give us some feedback. Also, could you tell your friends and neighbors to come try us out? We open on ..."

6. You becoming more comfortable with your own role and more confident in your management team.

While I don't want to scare you, there is no end to the depth and breadth
of things that can GO wrong. For example, we had a young man completely
blank on how to use the point of sale system. And while we stepped in to
handle the situation and worked to help him become more prepared for
the grand opening, he simply walked out. Had we waited until the grand
opening, the issue would have occurred in front of a long line of customers
all wondering what happened and watching him walk out. The situation
would have left you embarrassed and short-staffed—circumstances you'll
want to avoid.

Another employee, who was new to the industry and in her first full-time
job, simply lost it when faced with a stressful situation that was unlike
anything she had seen in training. Abandoning the customer, she went to
the breakroom in tears causing increased tension among employees and
heightened concern from clients—all of which would have been magnified
many times during GO. Fortunately, she accepted our coaching, returned
to her post and became a well-respected and confident employee.

During one soft opening, we discovered that the locals had no idea what
services we offered. So, we made an extra effort to help the clients understand our value. This effort led to longer service times which compounded
the staffing shortage we were already experiencing. Luckily, this experience occurred during a soft opening allowing us to make the adjustments
necessary for GO.

OPENING DAY (OR ALL-HANDS-ON-DECK DAY)

Everything you have done for the past few months (or years) has led up to this day. Blood, sweat, tears and lots of money have led you to this point. Do not squander this opportunity. Make some magic happen for you and your family today.

Typically, we schedule a couple of our top people to help us out on GO day. They provide customer service, fix problems with the point of sale or tools, talk to customers, run errands, whatever it takes to make a go of it. And without fail, we schedule ourselves (this is you) and our family to work. We ask them to arrive early, greet customers and support staff.

The night before a GO, we place our cheater signs, put out our banners and flags in front of our store, make sure our wrapped vehicles are parked strategically and conduct a run-through if we've hired a mascot or sign waver. On GO day, we ask our staff to be there an hour before opening to ensure they're completely prepared and at ease when we open the door.

No matter what you do on GO day:

Do NOT bail out early.

Do NOT take a long lunch.

Do NOT disappear in the middle of the day.

Do NOT pass GO or your responsibility to it.

Being in the heat of the battle will gain you so much status with the staff, and by extension the clients if they see you there working all day long. Your job is to make sure the last client of the day gets the same level of service delivered with the same enthusiasm as the first client of the day.

As the owner–operator you're not only the chief cook and bottle washer, you're also the lead cheerleader. When your staff gets tired, their enthusiasm wanes and they reach the point that they just want the day to be over, it's your job to provide them the energy they need to make it to the end of the day.

The last item on your GO checklist is to prepare to do the same thing tomorrow—and the day after. That's right, you will be back. This is your life now and your business. Your staff and customers will need you tomorrow just as much as they needed you today.

Now that your grand opening is in high gear, let's talk about expansion.

SPOTLIGHT: THE BAKER, LAUREL WILLIAMS

Bakers are not the type who usually come to mind when you think entrepreneur, but they are. Bakers are scrappy, small business owners who manage to stay upright by walking a tight rope, balancing between large equipment investments and staff, with long hours and low profit margins. Yet somehow, they make it work. Laurel Williams is a born entrepreneur who learned the art of small business from an unlikely source.

"My parents were missionaries, and they had a vision for a self-supporting Bible school. They bought a piece of property in the mountains of Colombia, South America, where I was born and raised," says Laurel. Her father learned all about coffee farming and before long, the farm supported several missionary families, a school for missionary kids and the free Bible school which included high school for Colombian students. The farm, Carmelo, trained a generation of Colombian pastors. Beyond that, Laurel's father went on to help start the very idea of giving small loans (also called micro-loans) to local entrepreneurs in South and Central America.

"There are a number of people who became incredibly wealthy in Colombia who got their first business training from my dad," she says, "He really believed that if you gave somebody a chunk of money and taught them how to use it wisely, they would prosper."

It worked well and he went on to help others start micro-loan programs all over the world. But when it was time to leave the nest, Laurel chose a different path. "I went off to college with no intention of ever being an entrepreneur." After graduating, she landed at a Fortune 100 medical supply company where she enjoyed stints in everything from HR to sales and finally, marketing. She learned all aspects of business, but after getting married took a hiatus.

"I was working all the time and decided that I would be at home and raise my kids instead." Her husband Dion had a good job and he held on to it as the kids grew, but never fit into the corporate culture. Before long, both felt unfulfilled. Dion channeled his energy into baking, which soon became his passion. When they decided to open a business, it was only natural that baking was at the top of the list. Why? Three reasons: "Number one he's an amazing pastry chef and has a heart for that. Number two it's a business that we could do together. Three, it offered the freedom for me to be creative on things I love like coffee and tea and hospitality and how we approached our customer service."

Again, her broad business experience translated well to the world of small business owner. Together, Laurel and Dion bought a Great Harvest franchise and haven't looked back. The challenges are big, especially keeping good staff because, "People don't realize that it's really hard work!" Laurel says.

Laurel soon learned that the amount of capital truly required to start and operate a franchise is far more than the cost of the franchise license, something she had not initially anticipated. Like everything in life, it always costs more than you think. But their ZOR helped them every step of the way, providing lots of support, training and flexibility.

At one point not long after opening, a construction project next door erected a seven-foot barricade that made their store look like it was closed from the street! "We lost one-third of our business, overnight," says Laurel. But with loans from family, a staff that pulled together like family and a franchisor who let them forgo some royalty payments, they managed to hang on and thrive. Despite the challenges, Laurel and Dion wouldn't trade it for a corporate corner office.

Her best advice? "If you plan on spending X amount of money on starting a business, double it and you'll be fine." In other words, it takes a lot of dough to run a bakery franchise.

CHAPTER 10:
OPERATIONS

n this chapter, you will learn the operating principles of a people-powered enterprise. *Akers of Advice* continues Jerry's call to prioritize operations excellence at every stage of franchise development, including
a potential expansion. *The Big Idea then* describes some of the items to
include in your own operational agenda: goal setting, periodic performance
reviews, staffing and recruiting tactics, best practices for training and
retaining top talent and expansion pros and cons.

AKERS OF ADVICE: BEST PRACTICE OPTIMIZATION

You You built a fully staffed operation, conducted a top notch soft open
and GO. You are in business. Now it's time to sit back, flip the switch and
let your business-in-a-box work its magic. Autopilot engage! Right?

Since you've made it this far, you know the answer. Your work has just
begun. Without continuous and unyielding focus on operational excellence, your GO success will quickly evaporate, leaving you wondering if it
was all just a dream.

Over the years, my family and I have built scores of franchise units from
the ground up and turned around dozens of units acquired from other
operators. While the circumstances and motivations of each acquisition

differed, one factor remained consistent—these businesses were not as successful as they could have been if they'd improved the quality of their operations. The math is simple. Without building a top-notch operation, you will never optimize the performance of your business, period. Too many ZEEs struggle to survive, or worse they quit without understanding how close they were to achieving real success.

The key to optimizing franchise success is dogged focus on operational excellence and an unyielding commitment to understanding new issues and challenges. I've seen franchisees clean up low-performing operations by simply asking unsatisfied customers why they were unsatisfied, correcting the issues raised and then sincerely asking those customers for a second chance. As simple as it sounds, these efforts often reinvigorate the business. Because operational excellence isn't a matter of will or mental and emotional commitment, it takes clearly established and communicated operational goals and the structure and discipline of an operational agenda.

THE BIG IDEA: THE OPERATIONS AGENDA

Time is money, but time and money aren't the same. We can always make more money, but time is finite and continuously diminishing. No single factor is more important to the success of your business than time and your use of it. How you and your staff choose to spend time will, in many ways, determine the success of your business. Goal setting is one of the best ways to get the most out of your time, every day.

Let's say winter is coming and the new year is fast approaching. You decide your annual goals and announce them to coincide with the start of the new year. What you do next will determine if your goals set the tone of your business for the next 12 months or are quickly forgotten, like so many New Year's resolutions. You share your goals and your vision for achieving them with the staff. You've broken down steps so that each role, functional area, geography or unit understands what they need to contribute to make it all come together.

Establishing goals is the easy part. Execution—that's hard! Anyone can paint a picture of a rosy tomorrow. Getting your team to follow that vision takes communication, determination, faith in your staff and the largest dose of leadership you can muster.

LEAD ON

Whether you feel it or not, your team is watching you. They are constantly asking themselves if you really mean what you say, if the goals you've set are real or just talk. It's up to you to lead.

AUTHENTICALLY CONNECT

Seek out opportunities to connect, credit and celebrate individual contributions to drive the bottom line. Most people, even in smaller companies don't mentally connect what they do with the big picture—acknowledge them and honor their efforts.

ROLL UP YOUR SLEEVES

Participate in the processes you've asked others to adopt. Your team wants to know that what you've asked is achievable and that you're willing to do it, too—show them you are.

MODEL THE WAY

Doing something once, may get you some attention. Doing it continually will help you nurture the behaviors you seek.

LET GO OF YOUR EGO

Get in the habit of regularly reviewing your progress and always be open to change. Adjusting your goals or admitting a goal wasn't right is an act of strength, not weakness.

ASK TOUGH QUESTIONS

Are we on pace to make our goal? What's working and what's not? Has anything in the market changed? Are our annual goals still relevant? What are our pain points (staffing, cashflow, inventory)?

DON'T LEAVE YOUR STAFF BEHIND

Always remember that your staff won't see the goals the same way you do. Just because you've seen the numbers and have a sense of what needs to change, your staff may not. More importantly, it's likely that the numbers don't really tell the tale and your staff may have insights and perspectives you haven't considered. It's also important to remember that individual contributors often struggle to make the connection between a big goal and what they do every day.

KEEP YOUR GOALS IN SIGHT

Annual goals take a long time to achieve and are often difficult to relate to the day in front of you. You can shorten the time between goal setting and goal getting through periodic check-ins. Take a timeout and get some Zzzs.

GET SOME ZZZS

Integrated into competition at every level is the chance to take a break, regroup and adjust to changing conditions. Football and basketball games include built-in, end-of-quarter and halftime breaks and each team gets a certain number of timeouts that can be deployed as needed. Why then do so many business owners allow themselves to be driven through entire business cycles without taking the time to analyze progress and modify their game plans to meet the changing needs of the market?

It's too easy to get caught up in the flow, to let the world set the pace of your business—but you are a TEMPO-setter, you can call the plays in your business. One of the most productive plays a franchise operator can call is timeout. At a minimum, we suggest calling a timeout for half-year reviews.

Gain ground on your competitors. Avoid your own mid-year doldrums. Almost all businesses struggle to keep employees engaged during the summer. The heat, family vacations, seasonal downturns in business and back-to-school distractions generally diminish productivity. While still protecting your own vacation, downtime and sanity, you can use this time to reignite your operation. While your competition is coasting, you'll be adding 30–60 days of productivity.

A mid-year analysis examines your annual goals with respect to your half-year performance. If you're running ahead of plan, you may want to adjust your goals upward. Conversely if you've fallen significantly behind, it may be time to reconsider your goals. When your review uncovers great performance, or you catch someone doing the right things—celebrate! It is impossible to overstate the power of simple, sincere gratitude and public acknowledgement of an employee's good work. It's cost-free and highly valuable, so use it.

Mid-year reviews are a great way to get your staff back in the game—even when it seems like there's a lot of game left to play. Taking time to review and reflect is a great way to re-energize yourself as well. Yes, you are human too and subject to your own ups and downs. Mid-year checkups can be just what the doctor ordered to refocus and revitalize your own performance.

ALWAYS BE RECRUITING

You are fully staffed, so you can stop recruiting, right? Not so fast. Just because you filled your staff requirements doesn't mean you can stop your recruiting efforts. Few things in franchise operation are more predictable than employee attrition. You'll often be working with younger staff who are just starting their professional careers. They move often and are always on the lookout for bigger and better opportunities, creating gaps in your staff roster. Also common are employees who are frequently tardy or those who miss shifts. These employees are typically underperformers and have trouble fitting into the team environment needed to run a small business.

While employee turnover is expected, there are ways to determine if the turnover you are experiencing is too high. Ask questions. Stop by a few of the other businesses in your complex and ask them what the churn is like in their businesses. Reach out to your ZOR and ask what the employee turn is like for similar units within your franchise system.

Once you know the standards, do everything in your power to stay ahead of the curve. The labor pool is the smallest it has been in years and candidates have many options. The trick is to become an *employer of choice*—the place everyone wants to work.

BECOME AN EMPLOYER OF CHOICE

Recruitment must be a planned, continuous activity because a short-staffed business simply can't provide the same level of service and personal attention as a fully staffed business. Clients have little patience for slow service caused by staffing issues so this should be a strong focus for you.

Today's applicants have a much different list of expectations and benefits than previous generations. Before recruiting from these groups, understand what they may be looking for and decide if you are willing to provide those things. More flexible hours and scheduling or even remote work options, relaxed dress codes and the chance to be part of an organization that is environmentally focused and socially sensitive are firm pluses. Of course, payrate and benefits are still likely to be at or near the top of the list, but advancement, career path and training opportunities can be powerful attractors.

TRAINING

In our experience, the modern applicant is probably looking for more than just a job. The problem is that the range of candidate expectations seems ever expanding. While you may not be able to keep up with the latest employee desires, there are several high-value benefits that employees want—sometimes even when they don't know they want or value them. Case in point—training.

Jerry and I have developed some of the most sophisticated and effective training programs in the business. Our training business not only supplements the courses and support offered by our ZORs but fills a gap that ZORs can't. As you may recall, in Chapter 7 we discussed a few of the reasons ZORs must keep distance between them and the employees or run the risk of being considered the de facto employer—something no one wants. The result is that ZORs don't generally provide as much training and support for employees. In fact, the need for quality training is so great that we've delivered our training programs outside of franchising to hundreds of the world's leading organizations.

If we are competing for a new hire and offer a training program that the candidate believes will help him or her develop faster than their peers, it may well be the difference maker. We don't just offer training to help them do their current job better, but training that will prepare them for their next job (hopefully with you).

Training can be provided by you and your staff or outsourced to a company like ours. It may be based on actual classes or readings, in-person or virtual. As the leader of your organization, take note of the employees who value training because your best employees will be interested in advancing themselves. Training will strengthen your operation, enhance employee skills and build leadership bench strength by preparing more employees to take on roles of progressively greater responsibility.

From our general managers to our newest employee, every member of our team has a role to play and a contribution to make. If we do our job right and we do right by our employees, we can help them assume larger roles and make larger contributions. That is the very definition of a win-win opportunity. Our slate of training options emphasizes five key areas of development.

1. Management Training—Attracting and training frontline staff is an ongoing challenge to franchise operators, as is building a pipeline of management prospects to fill out your executive team and support future growth opportunities.

2. Relationship Building and Networking—Building your business means more than exchanging your goods or services for some amount of revenue. Great businesses are built on customer service, personalized attention and human connection. People want to be part of something greater than themselves, to share an experience with others, to contribute to creating something new. Playing a game on the playground, working on a group project, supporting the local sports team as they march toward the title are just a few examples of how our lives revolve around connection. Great businesses know that customer service isn't only about facilitating

a transaction, but making connections that bind customers to your business on a personal level and allow them to become an extended member of your business family.

3. Value Based Selling—An approach that focuses on finding ways to benefit customers at every step of the sales process. Rather than sell to customers, we train our employees to guide customers through the sales process and help customers make an informed decision. Value based selling is a difference maker because people rarely buy products, but instead, convenience and solutions to problems or experiences. People don't purchase insurance; they purchase peace of mind and the feeling of safety knowing they'll be protected should the unexpected occur. Diners don't just patronize restaurants for the food; they enjoy the environment, the ambiance and the change of pace from eating at home. People are social animals that value unique experience, ritual and congregation. That's why we provide intensive value-based selling courses that teach our employees how to identify opportunities to generate customer value whenever possible.

4. Relationship Development—We build people-powered businesses—that means we treat our employees with respect and make every effort to get to know them as individuals. Our relationship development training teaches our employees to do the same thing with each customer. From connecting through small talk to building customer databases to help them remember customer details, like birthdays and other special occasions, our training seeks to transform transactions into meaningful relationships.

5. Home Budgeting—You may be asking yourself if you read that right. What does home budgeting have to do with our franchise business? This training is a direct result of learning everything we can about the profile of our employees. One of our franchise businesses is staffed largely by younger women who are just starting out in business and in life. We offer the course to help them understand basic financial planning in hopes that the experience will make them more successful and stable in their career with us. After helping them learn about home budgeting, these employees are much more likely to understand and capitalize on small bonus opportunities and sales programs we run. For example, examining customer revenue data, Jerry discovered that if a customer service representative who is paid a small bonus for each customer they service, helps one additional customer each hour then that representative could increase their salary by nearly 15%.

Each of these is designed to not only educate employees for our business, but for their lives. As their lives improve, they recognize the business created that for them and they tend to plan on staying with us for a very long time. This leads to better trained and motivated staff taking care of our customers and reduces recruiting and training time and expense in the future.

CUSTOMER SERVICE

Your staff and the way they interact with your customers will determine your business success. No matter which products or services your business provides, customers will demonstrate how well you do what you do by voting with their dollars. They will choose to either be loyal customers or one-time visitors. Customers look at the employee as a representative of the business. The service rendered by the employee reflects the operation's standards. Therefore, if a customer gets poor service from an employee at your business, it is common for the customer to blame the business rather than the individual. That's why customer service must be at the top of your priority list for staff. When evaluating potential new hires, focus on the people who demonstrate customer service skills before you hire them. Once they're onboard help them fine-tune these skills. Jerry often reminds me that he can teach any capable person how to do a given job, but he cannot teach people how to smile and interact with others in a comfortable and confident way. When you are in hiring mode, keep your eye out for friendly, outgoing types that aren't afraid to smile and exhibit an upbeat, positive demeanor.

Despite generational stereotypes suggesting younger workers are not willing to make the same sacrifices for work that their parents did, top performers of all ages are out there. It is your job to find and develop them.

RETENTION

Retention is an essential element to building a successful franchise operation. Make it a key area of focus for you and your organization. Today, people change jobs with greater frequency than ever before. As a franchise operator you can't turn the tide on the job-hopping phenomenon, but you can buck the trend one employee at a time.

The keys to employee retention are simple. Stay engaged with your staff by training others to act in your place and act as you would (treating others with respect and modeling the way). Catch people doing the right thing and acknowledge them for it. And ensure that the success of the business is shared by all who created it. It is important to find out what your employees think about the company, compensation and benefits. This information will lead to a better understanding of what it will take for you to continue to retain current staff. Surprisingly, much of what it takes to retain employees isn't very costly and wouldn't take much time to implement. Small performance bonuses, promotions or even special training opportunities are minor things that can make a major impact on lowering employee churn.

Appreciation is directly tied with job satisfaction. Jerry holds an annual employee appreciation event he calls the Celebration of Excellence party. This is a large event put on in a hotel ballroom with food, drinks, entertainment, prizes and performance awards, but the real value comes from the simple act of acknowledging employee effort and accomplishment and showing your staff how much you value them

CHAPTER 11:
AVOIDING CHAPTER 11

This chapter represents a departure, a deviation from the pattern and structure of our conversation. Until now, we've focused on the discovery, evaluation, selection, staffing, launch and operation of your new franchise business. Here, Jeff and Jerry give way to Ron Gardner, one of franchising's top legal advisers. Ron reveals an unspoken truth and what could be a fatal flaw hidden deep within the franchise journey. The chapter concludes with Schlotzsky's franchise owner Albert Shelton's *Spotlight* that proves the existence of life after franchise death.

SPOTLIGHT: THE DEFENDER, RON GARDNER

Hollywood storytelling has conditioned us to believe that the stories of good people, pure of heart and motivated by family and hope, always turn out alright in the end. *Live It 2 Own It* is the story of you. Throughout, we've assumed you are a good person, you follow the rules, eat your vegetables and are kind to children and small animals. In this story, you've made a bet on yourself and being the selfless person that you are, your only motivation was to build a stable financial future for you and your family. Implicit in this Hollywood tale is that it will lead straight to a happy ending.

Reality. [Enter stage, right]

Reality, where the unexpected cuts through hopes, dreams and good intentions like a knife through butter. Such is the reality of franchise ownership. You could do everything right, follow every step and process in this book and still fail to build a sustainable franchise business.

If your Hollywood ending eludes you and you find yourself with a failed business and a long-term commitment to pay fees and royalties to a ZOR that has a contractual right to expect, demand and even take legal action to ensure these fees are paid, you'll need the help of a man no one ever wants to meet. Ron Gardner is a nice guy, the kind of person most people would love to hang out with. He's funny, personable and genuinely cares about people, especially people with franchise troubles. The problem is that by the time you meet him, it might be too late to save your business. Ron Gardner isn't the franchise doctor, he's one of the top franchise dispute lawyers in the business—the defender.

When a ZEE is about to lose their life savings and reputation, Gardner steps in and cleans up what's left of a business with a clever and astute approach.

Growing up Ron never dreamed of being a lawyer. In fact, he didn't have much time to dream. His family was poor and at one point, his mother, father and two brothers all lived in their only asset—a car. After a series of demeaning jobs, his father's frustration grew so fierce he turned to the bottle. His parents divorced soon after and Ron and his brothers stayed with their mother while she worked two jobs. Money was so scarce they sacrificed heating their home to keep food on the table. Despite these challenges, Ron did well in school. And teachers took note of his potential. Looking past Ron's hand-me-down clothes, one teacher proved a particularly strong influence—his debate coach. Ron had an uncanny combination of natural smarts and verbal skills that made him an excellent debater.

A college scholarship, marriage, a short stint as a radio announcer and a series of fruitless jobs led Gardner to pursue a law degree. Working day and night, Ron passed the bar and found a job as a clerk in a new firm in Minneapolis. One of the partners of a large prestigious firm invited Ron to join a new boutique firm he was starting that would be dedicated to franchise law. Gardner was keen to join him but had one condition—he only wanted to represent the little guys, the franchisees. It's not that Ron saw ZORs as the enemy. It was his upbringing, the struggles he experienced that motivated him. His passion was for Mom & Pop owners. People that bought a franchise with dreams of being entrepreneurs, only to realize they'd made a mistake, didn't have the skills to operate a franchise business or simply didn't understand the fine print. As Gardner saw it the deck was stacked against the ZEEs, the remediation process lopsidedly in favor of the ZORs. More importantly, Ron wanted to figure out ways to keep ZEEs out of his office by advocating on behalf of owner–operators.

So how do you keep your business from needing legal intervention? At the first sign of trouble see a doctor—a franchise advisor to help identify early warning signs and stop them before they become more serious issues. Ron advises, "Don't ignore those signs. If things aren't going well, it could be you're not working the system correctly, or the system itself is flawed." When you see those signs, get help before it's terminal. A professional advisor will assess your situation and give you the cold, hard facts.

Gardner says it's never too early to be thinking about the possibility of franchise failure, not to discourage small business owners but to ensure they've thought through all the possibilities. Before committing funds to a hot new franchise, or a settled one, you've got to decide if the risk is worth the rewards. "Ask yourself, am I an entrepreneur or not?" says Ron. That is the first step. You can think about buying a franchise like buying your first car. Do you remember that experience? Pumped up on the potential of newfound freedom, you weren't as concerned about financing options, insurance costs, maintenance and other incidentals as you might be buying a car today. Back then, you just wanted that shiny new toy that could take you to all the places you couldn't go before. It was an emotional decision, and emotional decisions are often made without the due diligence necessary to make the right choices.

Keep your eyes and your options open. If one franchise is not a good fit, move on because there's more at stake than the money you've already invested. Depending on the structure of your agreement, even if your franchise fails, you will likely be bound to pay lost royalties or other fees for months or years into the future. To avoid franchise failure, select a top shelf franchisor with a solid business model and a track record of providing quality franchisee support.

Just as a surgeon wouldn't discourage people from seeing a cardiologist to monitor and guide them through heart issues, Ron encourages ZEEs to seek out the help and assistance of lawyers. "I would be out of business if people used lawyers earlier in the process. My phone only rings when things are in near ruin. I want them to be successful. What drives me is the enormous feeling of accomplishment when I can help people avoid the pending disaster. The law is slow and cumbersome and painful, and nobody really wins," Ron explains.

"People call me because they are mad or scared. Then in two-and-a-half years when we finally get a resolution, they shift their anger to me because it has taken them so much time. It is an unshakeable feeling even when they've gotten a million dollars rather than losing everything. I now do much more negotiating and represent a lot of associations," he adds.

Ron serves on a committee called the North American Securities Administrators Association, the trade group for state regulators that oversees the sale of franchises. He wants to ensure potential ZEEs get the information they need to avoid being defrauded or being bound to restrictions that often limit a ZEE's ability to salvage part of their investment by selling their franchise license to someone else.

Interestingly, Ron categorizes entrepreneurs and passive investors as higher risk ZEEs. Entrepreneurs differ from the typical business operator in that they are more willing to take risks and seek quick returns. Passive investors often believe they can simply turn the reins of the business over to other people and just show up occasionally to collect their profits. "I am often asked if a franchisee is an entrepreneur. There is no clear line or right answer on that, only observations. Entrepreneurs who are a little less risk adverse or see a way to get from 0–60 faster, will often take the bait of franchising. There is an equal number of people who fall completely for the cliché, 'You have a partner every step of the way. Just bring your 401K.'" Ron's advice aligns with that of longtime franchise executive Peter Holt, President and CEO of The Joint Chiropractic, who says, "Franchising is a business model that rewards patience and hard work."

Studies report that by the age of 55, about one in three doctors will be sued for malpractice. Doctors with better patient relationships are far less likely to be sued. Similarly, Gardner believes that relationships, how ZORs treat and engage with ZEEs, is a big part of why franchisees end up in his office. The most successful franchisors—in terms of whether Gardner's phone rings or not—are those who treat franchisees as if they are their most important investors. Even though franchisees aren't shareholders and cannot vote to remove anyone from the board or impact share price or performance by selling their shares, they treat them as if they could. They listen. Ron estimates he'd see a 50% case load reduction if ZORs, "just listened to what the franchisee had to say. The number one frustration I see is a lack of empowerment. They bought in and believed. They were ready to make a difference but now their opinion somehow does not matter and they're not being heard. Successful franchises empower their franchisees and allow them to help drive the brand."

Ron advises franchisees to keep alert to what the franchisor is doing and why. It's a red flag when rather than being the systematic, data-driven analysts you went into business with, your ZOR starts making uncharacteristic or sudden changes, like deciding to rebrand the whole system, move from bricks and mortar to the internet, eliminate company stores or introduce entirely new products without a logical rationale or broad-based franchisee support. Top-down edicts don't sit well with people who invested their life savings to break free from the constraints of corporate America. "All because they didn't listen and didn't do their homework," Ron says.

Gardner estimates that 10–15% of his case load involves ZEEs with about one year of tenure, or people who bought into an existing license and have never met their ZOR. Franchisee claims generally fall into three buckets.

FRONT-IN CLAIMS

These claims center on the belief that the franchisee was defrauded by requiring the ZEE to invest more than agreed or expected, or the franchisee failing to experience an expected return.

DURING THE LIFECYCLE CLAIMS

These claims come from the belief that the franchisee did not receive the support they thought they'd get. Also, in this category are encroachment claims. These claims deal with the sale of franchise licenses to new operators that are believed to be too close to existing franchisees, thus diminishing the potential profitability of both.

TERMINATION

Franchise licenses secure the right to own and operate a franchise business in a specific geography for a specific time. At the end of the period, typically a decade or so, the ZEE must renew the license, paying a fee much like they did when they first became a ZEE. For the most part, the renewal process is fairly straightforward and because the business has been up and running for an extended period, the process isn't too cumbersome. However, for any number of reasons, the ZOR may choose to deny a renewal or disallow a license transfer that occurs near the end of the original term. A situation that, as you might imagine, is fraught with emotion and anxiety.

SPOTLIGHT: THE RESPIRATOR, ALBERT SHELTON

Franchise owners struggle to squeeze as many hours into a day as possible, internalize every deadline and personally approve every decision. Others take the laissez-faire (or let it be) approach, assuming the staff will address such things. Our advice? Avoid both ends of the spectrum. You have a staff, you've trained them well, let them do their jobs, but stay intimately engaged in the workings of your business, because no one knows or cares more about your business.

Albert Shelton, who owns a chain of Schlotzsky's sandwich shops, offers his perspective, "One of my fellow shop owners had a great store. Everyone loved it. Great location and sales, but he was letting it run itself while he was out playing golf. Meanwhile, one of his managers stole $100,000 from him. So from that point on, he micro-managed every aspect. He was there from open to close seven days a week. His nerves were shot, he neglected his family and it almost drove him out of the business before he learned to trust and delegate again." Albert was determined not to let that happen to him, but it wasn't easy.

"Most franchise owners, like many small business owners, will work themselves harder than any boss could ride them. When you own your own business, it's always on your mind," he says. Albert admits that it's still hard for him to let go and give his employees decision-making power. "To give someone the authority to do things without my thumbprint all over it, yeah, that's tough. I learned that it squashes their creativity when you hand them a project and then micro-manage every detail." It not only hurts productivity but profitability as well.

Albert learned this lesson early in his work life, but it didn't carry over into his franchising experience. "I started as a respiratory therapist after college. I moved up in the company to head a department and learned how to manage people. It was good, but after a while not very challenging. I tried my hand at pharmaceutical sales, but still I yearned to have my own business," says Albert.

Shelton bought an ill-timed computer sign-making franchise that failed as quickly as personal computers that could do the same thing (only much cheaper) became commonplace. It was a serious blow that caused sleep-less nights and nearly cost Albert and his young family their home. "I didn't smile for three years," says Albert. He went back to respiratory therapy for a while before opening yet another small business, cleaning and restoring expensive wooden decks and fences. He could finally breathe again, and it boosted his entrepreneurial confidence.

That's when the universe stepped in to change his life forever. Albert was eating in a Schlotzsky's franchise and struck up a conversation with the owner, who complained about not being able to add more locations because he had no one to run them. "I felt like life was tapping me on the shoulder. So, I asked him if he'd be interested in taking on a partner," says Albert. Soon after, Albert bought a third of the business, eventually became the sole owner then added a Cinnabon franchise (which is run by the same ZOR as Schlotzsky's). Shelton's businesses were profitable, and that profit was sustainable. Albert had arrived at the destination he'd fought so hard for.

Reflecting on his experience, Shelton has two pieces of advice for potential ZEEs—money and location. "Not having enough money in the bank is the number one franchise killer," says Albert adding, "but don't go heavily into debt either. Once you're able to secure a line of credit, only use it when you have no other choice. Save your money." Shelton shares his cash-in-the-bank admonition with anyone who's thinking about starting a franchise. He then adds his second piece of advice, "Bad site selection will kill you. That's one of the worst mistakes you can make. I've seen more than a couple of stores around us close within a few years, all because of weak locations. So choose well."

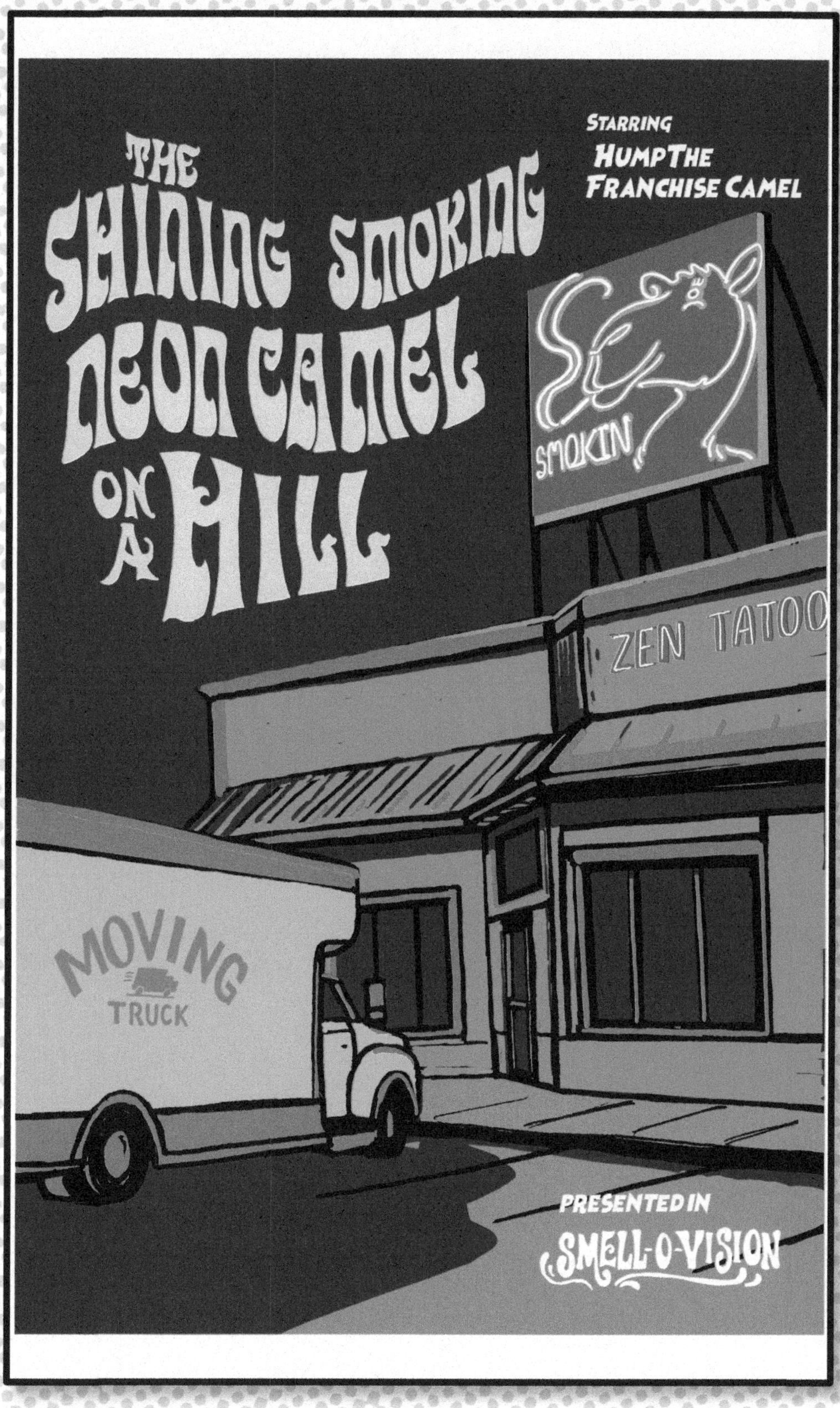
THE SHINING SMOKING NEON CAMEL ON A HILL
STARRING
HUMP THE FRANCHISE CAMEL
SMOKIN
ZEN TATOO
MOVING TRUCK
PRESENTED IN
SMELL-O-VISION

CHAPTER 12:
TO EXPAND OR NOT TO EXPAND

his chapter explores the opportunities and challenges associated with franchise expansion. *Akers of Advice* recounts Jerry's personal journey from single-shingle business to multi-brand, multi-state, multi-unit operation. *The Big Idea* then examines the benefits and drawbacks of organic and inorganic expansion activities. *Spotlight* completes the discussion by introducing former franchise coach Katie Yeargan, who explains the value a franchise coach can bring to your business.

AKERS OF ADVICE: A SHINING CAMEL ON A HILL

ZEEs often ask me, "How long should I operate my first unit before thinking about expansion?"

My response is consistent and unequivocal. "That all depends."

Universally unsatisfied with my answer, a second question invariably follows. "How long did it take you, Jerry? "

The problem is that they are asking patient-old-warrior Jerry a question about something impatient-man-child Jerry did and thought long ago. I see the expectation in their eyes, awaiting a guru-like thunderclap of insight.

Although I've yet to work up the nerve, my dream response would sound like something David Carradine would have said in the 70's TV show Kung Fu. "To find my expansion truth, I first needed to expand my mind. I moved to a mountain top and waited there for 1,000 years. Until the day I saw the light, a shining light atop a distant hill. I grabbed the pebbles from my master's hand sure in the knowledge that it was time for me to GO." Pause for effect. Let it sink in and finish with, "This you must now do. GO my child."

Truth be told, I was making expansion plans before the ink was dry on my franchise license. Once I'd made the decision to become a franchise operator, I was all-in and ready for more. Ready except for one pesky little problem—reality. Mickey and I were still working full-time jobs while building our business. We had to learn how the business operated. We had to learn how to make the business profitable, survive downturns and find a work-life balance that would protect us from burning out. Yet, none of those things compared to my biggest challenge. I had to work up the nerve to ask the love of my life, the woman I'd just convinced to jump headfirst into a business we knew literally nothing about, if she'd double down and be willing to raise the stakes and multiply the risk to a level many times that which she'd agreed to only weeks before.

Amazingly, I found my nerve. More amazing, I discovered another example of why I'm a very, very lucky man. Mickey said, "Yes!" That was all I needed, because with Mickey on my side, no challenge is unattainable. Within three years, we'd grown our operation to five stores, largely through acquisition. That's when an amazing opportunity surfaced. An opportunity to enter a new market and open a new store in a dynamite location about 80 miles from our home.

Still, was it the right move?

Was it the right time?

Did we have the bandwidth and experience to take on more responsibility and risk?

I knew just where to turn.

THE FRANCHISE COACH

One of the best pieces of advice I've ever received was to enlist the help of a franchise coach, someone with the experience to help me navigate the hard decisions every ZEE must make. Whether you formally hire a professional coach or informally tap into the wisdom of a seasoned ZEE, being able to lean on an experienced operator is invaluable—one of the best investments a ZEE can make. If you follow this advice, a word of caution: A good coach will tell you what you need to hear, not what you want to hear—a reality some (control-freak entrepreneurs) may find uncomfortable.

FRED FLINTSTONE AND MR. SLATE

Flushed with excitement, I called my franchise coach and explained the opportunity. I was pushing hard, enthusiastically selling the benefits of the market and the location. Looking back, I now realize that I wasn't asking for a reasoned opinion, I was looking for permission, like a small boy seeking a parent's approval. My coach knew me better than I knew myself, he'd been there. After silently listening to my sales pitch, he suggested that Mickey and I had more to do and more to learn before we expanded further. He told us that we needed to slow down now to go faster later. As he spoke, I felt like Fred Flintstone, the cartoon character from The Flintstones. Whenever Fred did something wrong at work, his boss, Mr. Slate would get on the loudspeaker and call him into his office. Spitting mad, Slate would berate poor Fred about his behavior. Red- faced and ashamed Fred would inexplicably start shrinking. Physically shrinking. The more Slate yelled, the smaller Fred got. When Slate was all yelled out, a now one-inch-tall Fred would climb down from his chair and leave his boss's office—a mere fraction of the man he'd once been.

My coach wasn't the yelling type. He'd never say anything to hurt me or make me feel bad. But his advice made me feel like a one-inch-tall Jerry. Head down and mumbling to myself, I left the meeting a little smaller than when I'd entered.

I hadn't heard what I wanted to hear.

In fact, I heard the opposite of what I wanted to hear.

Worse yet, I heard the one word entrepreneurs never want to hear—NO!

Later, clear-headed again but still disappointed, I knew I was lucky to have the sage advice of a franchise pro. So instead of finding a way around the rules, instead of finding a way to ignore the advice I'd been given in favor of what I wanted to do (both go-to Jerry moves), I did something completely out of character. I listened and obeyed.

We passed on the deal.

Our competition did not.

In fact, my competition not only opened a store in that market, but they also took the prime location I'd discovered.

They say that time heals all wounds.

Not for me.

Months turned into years, and I still couldn't get over the one that got away. I wish I could tell you that the market and the location turned out to be a bust and that my competition left the market like Fred leaving Mr. Slate's office, but that simply wasn't the case. They had a great GO and proceeded to build a successful business on the southside of town.

Wait, what?

Like a thunderclap, a revelation revealed itself as a simple logical proof.

Given: Things have sides.

A city is a thing.

Therefore: A city has sides.

Our customers want convenience and value, they don't make appointments and certainly wouldn't travel across town for our service. So, while my competition continued to do well on one side of the city, the other side of town remained pristine, untapped and unserved.

I had waited, as I was advised to wait. I had learned what I was advised to learn. My operation was humming. I was hungry for more and knew without ever saying a word, I was back in the hunt.

Using my site selection tool kit (see Chapter 6: Select Your Site, *The Big Idea*) I soon learned that there was no existing commercial real estate inventory on the north side of town. A trip to the zoning board added more unwelcome news; the local government had issued a moratorium on commercial construction, so no new sites were under development, nor would there be for the foreseeable future. Worse still, my franchise agreement clearly stipulated that new units must be part of a multi-tenant shopping mall with either a national big box retail store or regional grocery chain as anchor tenant.

Time to get creative, Jerry. Time to not only think outside the box, but time to crush the box and burn the evidence. Rather than fight the rules, the new more mature Jerry asked better questions.

Why did my ZOR require franchise units be part of a multi-unit complex with specific types of anchor tenants?

If I could find an alternative solution that accomplished what those rules were designed to accomplish, I might have a shot.

The answer was simple.

My ZOR adopted the model because it effectively tapped into existing customer traffic patterns to make it easy for customers to stop in.

Armed with that knowledge, I did what any sane middle-aged man would do. I started cruising the mall parking lots and hanging out in my parked car. I was hard at work conducting a parking lot challenge (see Chapter 6: Selecting Your Site, *Activity*). I drove and parked. Drove and parked and counted cars. Every day. Day after day, for a week. Each day I drove at a different time. I compared the weekday traffic counts against weekend traffic counts. I counted the cars headed down the street and counted the cars headed up the street. It all paid off when I discovered a thoroughfare that was the only way into and out of a highly populated residential area. The thoroughfare led to the top of a hill, and on that hill, I saw a shining light and it beckoned me, "Jerry, go into the light!" And that's just what I did.

Guess I am getting a little older, because as I got closer my eyes reported a much different picture of what I'd seen. It wasn't just a light. It was a neon light. A purple neon light in the form of a smoking camel, and that light was adorning a tattoo parlor. It all took a second to sink in, and it produced a sinking feeling in the pit of my stomach. That's when I saw it, right there in the neon drenched tattoo parlor parking lot, I saw the most beautiful thing I'd seen in ages—a moving van. The prior tenants were moving out and the property hadn't been listed yet. Hmmm.

The tattoo parlor wasn't in a big mall, it was in a small strip center. The anchor tenant wasn't a big box store or grocery chain. Its anchor tenant was a national drug store. Looking out from the parking lot toward the street, my excitement mounted because traffic heading away from the city and toward people's homes was in the lanes closest to our parking lot. Customers would only have to make a right turn to end up at our future front door. The site offered premier visibility, traffic counts that rivaled the big mall on the other side of town and an anchor tenant that attracted as many customers as some of the traditional anchors.

I took a few pictures. Organized my data. Made a nice little binder and set out to convince my ZOR's real estate team to bend, wave and/or ignore the rules, just this once! Happy to listen and surprisingly open-minded, the real estate folks were impressed by the data and ultimately approved the construction of my non-conforming site.

The buildout came next and was so frustrating, with so many unexpected problems and delays, that I often wished the real estate folks had rejected my hair-brained scheme. The remodel required that we cut out several steel beams. If you've never had to cut out a steel beam, keep it that way. It is unfun! To my surprise we learned that the site had a tri-level floor. No, a tri-level floor isn't a floor style or feature, it is a problem. A big problem that costs a lot of money to fix. As a rule of thumb, floors should be flat and run across a single level. If a floor does not conform to these criteria you must pay to make it so. Moreover, the property had once been an old-style gas station, eye-catching but not exactly our brand's clean corporate look. Luckily, we only needed one thing to bring it into compliance —money. The interior boasted of seafoam green walls and tattoo tables that were welded to the floor. Smack-dab in the center of the space stood an enormous freestanding koi pond. Yep. A koi pond inside a tattoo parlor, inside an old-style gas station, atop a hill adorned by a giant, shining neon-purple, smoking camel.

Zen tat, anyone?

I'm very grateful that our franchise coach slowed me down. His advice gave Mickey and me the time we needed to build our existing territory and learn the business from the ground up. We opened the store, and it grew more quickly than any of our stores before it, partly because we'd become better franchise operators and partly because that store was truly my shining light on a hill.

So, should you expand?

That all depends.

THE BIG IDEA: WAYFINDING

To expand or not to expand, that is the question. ZEEs new to the expansion question generally believe that the only thing better than having a single thriving franchise unit is having two thriving franchise units. If two is better than one, then four must be better than two. By extension it follows that operating 40 thriving units must be downright wonderful. Not necessarily.

As Peter Holt mentioned in his opening remarks (see Foreword), franchising isn't an industry, it's a method for rapidly accelerating business model development—build, operate, optimize, duplicate and repeat. Expansion is an integral part of the franchise approach and a big part of the franchise culture. However, a simple fact remains. Expanding your business is not always a good idea. The effects of failed expansion efforts are seldom limited to the new units but instead negatively affect the entire operation.

The allure of empire building is strong in the growth steeped franchise culture, leading otherwise grounded businesspeople to surrender their practical and tactical approach in favor of the euphoric haze that comes with what we call jackpot thinking. Anytime a rational, consistently successful ZEE starts talking like the monocled Monopoly man and less like the steady operator they'd always been, it's time to worry. Jackpot thinking promises payouts so big that it's easy to ignore the risks and accept as fact conclusions born of flawed reasoning. This may be why it's so common to hear one of Jerry's coaching clients say, "I'm already running one successful location; it should be easy to add a few more," or "Running a handful of new stores can't be much different than what I'm doing right now." Unfortunately, these statements and others like them are incorrect.

We have seen far too many successful ZEEs, people with comfortable incomes and lifestyles they enjoy, make the decision to expand—only to regret it. Expansion activities are never a sure thing. Expansion is a complicated, life-altering decision that can deliver your greatest dreams or unleash your worst nightmares. Expansion isn't just a matter of your readiness to operate more stores or your ability to invest the additional capital necessary to build and equip new locations. Even the consummate operator, flush with cash and raring to go, must be willing to put in the time necessary to find a location, manage the buildout and hire staff. Expanding ZEEs must be patient enough to wait for the day the business finally tips the scales and moves from money pit to money maker—and be mentally, emotionally and financially prepared in case that day never comes.

The best way to start the process is to understand what expansion is and what it is not. Expansion isn't a choice, it's an outcome. Is your expansion goal to generate more revenue? More customers? Open more physical locations? Or all three? Whatever your answer, there's an expansion strategy to help you accomplish your goal. For purposes of this discussion, we'll explore three forms of expansion: organic, inorganic and diversification.

ORGANIC EXPANSION

One of the earliest mentions of the term organic growth dates back to the 1899 book, *The Soul of Japan*, which described the country's modernization. The term evolved to mean business growth resulting from improvements to existing business operations, including productive output, customer reach and the introduction of new products. Given this understanding, we strongly believe ZEEs should be continuously engaged in organic expansion activities.

PROTECT AND GROW

Frank ran a small-town heating and air conditioning business, a thriving franchise operation for nearly 30 years. He had grown up in the business and loved to help on jobs, so he took every opportunity to tag along on service calls. With Frank in the field, operational tasks would go unattended for months on end. In other words, customers were not being billed for the work his company provided.

In parallel, Frank's small town was rapidly becoming a bedroom community for a growing city nearby. Frank's new customers had moved to the suburbs with high customer service expectations. Things like clean trucks, technicians who explained the problem, booties over the workers' shoes when indoors, prompt billing—all simple things, but things his company wasn't doing. During our analysis, we discovered these extras could potentially double his business in as little as two years if he trained his techs (and himself) to deliver these consistently. After six months of implementation, his business was on a double-digit growth trajectory.

But after our weekly meetings, Frank only temporarily refocused his efforts on leadership, training and accountability for his techs. He would stick to it for a couple days or so, then go back to service calls. The more time he spent in the field, the less time he focused on what would grow his company. Eventually his old habits led his revenues to fall back to pre-coaching levels. Soon, Frank was spending all his time in the field because he was the only employee left. That's when he hired his daughter Jenna and his son Nick. Jenna took over office operations and billing and Nick set out to win back their former customers, one account at a time. Within two years, Frank's new second-generation team had firmly established operating procedures, a great service program and more customers than ever. For Frank, Jenna and Nick, their expansion efforts were first a means of survival, then an excellent example of how to expand an existing operation.

Increased business output encompasses everything from elevating worker productivity levels to selling more of what you already offer to the customers you already serve. Expanding your customer base, working to increase the sheer number of customers your business serves is (or should be) the daily concern of every ZEE. Customer acquisition activities are a continuous and ongoing effort that includes local promotions and corporate brand marketing in partnership with the ZOR. And while new product development is the responsibility of your ZOR, there are ways for you to participate in this important expansion activity. Most franchise systems feature an advisory council or similar mechanism to provide ZEEs a platform from which to share concerns and provide feedback, including new product development.

You want the greenlight to expand right now? Expanding organically should be your goal every time you open your doors. Plans focused on generating organic growth are generally safer but offer smaller, incremental returns. Because organic expansion is an integrated part of existing operations, conducting organic expansion activities won't stretch your resources or your patience the way riskier expansion strategies can.

INORGANIC EXPANSION

At the other end of the expansion spectrum, inorganic growth strategies come with greater risk and potentially very-high returns. Inorganic growth is measured by the rate of business output growth, which results from mergers and acquisitions and takeovers. Inorganic expansion is especially attractive because it offers a form of instant gratification. Take Jane for example, she operates a single unit which generates revenue of $1 a day. She decides to acquire a second unit, which coincidentally also makes $1 a day. With this acquisition, Jane instantly doubled her revenue from $1 to $2 a day. On the surface, a great deal all around. The problem is there is no guarantee that the predicted acquisition benefits will materialize.

To illustrate the point, let's look a little deeper into the performance of Jane's stores. Her original unit generates $1 a day and spends $.75, yielding a tidy $.25 profit. The newly acquired unit generates the same $1 but spends $1.30, producing a daily $.30 loss. Before she made the acquisition Jane's business was humming along, generating a whopping 25% profit. With the addition of the new location, Jane is now having to manage a business that costs more money to operate than it makes in revenue. She's losing $0.05 every day ($0.25 profit plus $0.30 loss equals a loss of $0.05).

The cost of opening or acquiring new units is generally lower than the cost of opening your first unit. Having worked with many vendors during the development of your first location, you'll have a good understanding of who to call, what to expect and how to do things better, faster and cheaper the next time around. Your vendors will see that you are growing the business and that you are likely to grow even more in the future (see Chapter 2: The TEMPO Effect, for more on creating mutual support for mutual success). Your growth would mean more opportunity for your vendors as well, which is serious motivation for them to provide you with preferred pricing and expert advice—all of which can lower the cost of starting a new location and shortening the time it takes for the new unit to generate positive cash flow.

Multiple-unit operations can share in the cost of expenses not related to any single unit. This type of expense is referred to as overhead expense and includes things like owner's compensation, association memberships, general purpose vehicles or storage space. These expenses aren't attributable to any single unit but are shared among the units. Sharing or spreading overhead in this way generally leads to a lower overhead burden for each unit. For example, let's say you operate one unit with an overhead cost of $2 a month. You then open a second unit and decide to spread your overhead, each unit would only have to contribute $1 overhead per month.

While spreading your overhead improves unit cashflow positions (making positive cashflow more positive and negative cashflow less so), there is no way to avoid the need for cash in the development or acquisition of new units and the need for cash will continue until that unit's revenue exceeds the unit's need for cash. Will your banker give you a line of credit to cover your start-up and the lean months or years until your new unit generates more cash than it consumes?

A TALE OF TWO ZEES

Bob has a good life. He owns a sub sandwich shop that's been in the same location for a decade. He has a comfortable income and little stress. Bob relies on two seasoned managers to handle day-to-day operations. He comes into the shop a couple of times a week to chat with customers and staff, drop off paychecks and address any issues that need his attention.

Bob has no plans to expand.

Ever!

Even the idea of operating another location makes Bob feel stressed. He knows expansion would mean having to spend more time working on the business, but his biggest fear is having to delegate much of what he currently views as his job. Bob is happy and sees no reason to change things.

Gail is also an operator in the same franchise system as Bob. She runs 12 units. Her operation is profitable and well run. She visits each store about once a month, where she works at the counter, talks to customers and staff and spends one-on-one time with the unit manager to discuss any problems needing her attention.

Committed to service excellence, Gail retained a professional training company to ensure her staff is equipped with the best customer service training, tools and techniques. She enjoys a high income, is okay dealing with stress and has enough of a cash reserve to weather slower revenue periods. Gail is happy—especially when she's thinking about opening new locations. For her, there's nothing quite like a GO. She's entirely comfortable delegating day-to-day operations because her staff is experienced, trustworthy and well-trained.

In both situations the ZEEs are content because their operations align with their personal and professional goals. Each has differing comfort levels when it comes to stress, time commitment and task delegation. They have taken the same business model and tailored it to meet their unique needs.

In a multi-unit operation, individual unit performance will vary. Provided this variance is a temporary blip or understandable fluctuation and not the sign of a bigger problem, underperforming unit revenue shortfalls can be offset by the superior performance of other units. This strategy applies to new unit development, giving you the option to leverage the cash generated by profitable units to cover the shortfall of launching a new location. We strongly caution against building your operation using the leverage model because it's a fragile approach, one that puts your entire operation at risk should something go wrong.

DIVERSIFICATION

Diversification holds a unique place and meaning as applied to franchise expansion. Normally diversification is considered part of organic growth, because in a typical business the development of new products or services is the responsibility of the business that provides them. Not so with the franchise model that places responsibility for new product and service diversification squarely on the shoulders of the ZOR. However, this doesn't mean that ZEEs are left with no diversification options. As an independent businessperson you are free to invest in other franchise models. This approach is in stark contrast with inorganic growth in which expansion means operating multiple units of the same brand in different locations. Franchise diversification means operating multiple units of multiple brands in the same or differing geographies.

Brand diversification means surrendering some of the advantages associated with multi-unit operations, including the ability to leverage a fully trained staff. New brand. New service model. New and often different kinds of employees (cooks versus hairstylists).

However, multi-brand operations can provide an extra layer of protection in case of industry downturns. Let's say you operate a smoothie store and a small gym. The smoothie shop has a line around the block all summer long but doesn't see many customers when the temperatures turn frigid in the winter. Meanwhile the gym next door is empty in the summer when temperatures are high, and people want to be outside enjoying the sunshine but packed in the winter when there's less of an excuse to skip the gym. Unlike inorganic smoothing of revenues across multiple units operating the same brand model, diversification allows for performance balancing across multiple industries.

ACTIVITY: EXPANSION SELF-TEST

With no standards, no universally accepted processes to guide operators along the expansion journey, ZEEs are left alone to navigate a sea of data and advice. Exhausted and confused, convinced that the answer isn't out there, they turn inward and make a gut decision. A dice roll bet that promises payouts that are rarely realized. The kind of wager that built the billion-dollar properties that line the Las Vegas Strip. Good for the house. Not so good for the gambler.

The real question is how can you improve your odds? How can you move from gut feeling to logical rationale? The best way to answer these questions is to ask a few more. The activity for this chapter is simple. Take out five sheets of paper. At the top of each sheet, write out one of the following questions. Use the remainder of each page to write out your answer.

1. What are my income goals?

If your existing operation generates the income you desire, you may not want to risk what you have for the possibility of earning a few more dollars.

2. What are my lifestyle goals?

Finding a balance between work and life is a difficult task, a goal many people never achieve. What's your ideal lifestyle? How much are you working? How much are you playing? How close are you to achieving that goal right now? If you're comfortable with the way things are. If you have a successful business that generates predictable revenues and profit, a staff you can count on and a workload that gives you plenty of time for hobbies or other interests, are you willing to roll the dice and assume more responsibility and risk?

3. Will the expansion help or hinder your income and lifestyle goals?

It's true. Expanding your business is likely to increase your income, that's why so many operators do it. In fact, the franchise model is designed for inorganic growth. However, expansion success comes with a cost. Before you commit to an inorganic or diversification plan, it's wise to consider, deeply consider, the trade-offs, the personal and professional cost of building a bigger operation. Less personal time, greater financial pressure, mental and emotional stress are all part of the territory and need to be a part of your expansion calculation.

4. Are you willing to delegate?

Lots of single-shingle operators only need to look in the mirror to find the reason for their success. It's common for active and engaged owners to run the day-to-day operation. They become successful because they make all the decisions and do all the hard stuff themselves. A one-stop-operator approach works well for single unit operators that enjoy working in the business. Owners of multi-unit or multi-brand operations don't have that luxury—they must make the transition from working in the business to working on the business.

Multi-unit, multi-brand owners compelled to position themselves at the center of their operational universe, the sole source for decisions, the doer of all important tasks, are seldom effective leaders and risk mental and physical burn out. For some the issue isn't about control, it's about con-fidence. Many of the owners we've asked this question to candidly share that they are unsure about what to do, so don't feel comfortable putting someone else in that uncomfortable situation. If your need for control stems from a lack of self-confidence. Don't expand.

Take the time you need to learn the business from the ground up. When you start thinking that nothing new or unexpected ever seems to happen, when you start reacting instead of doubting, it will be time to reconsider the expansion question.

Inorganic and diversification efforts are a team sport. Winning teams are those best able to capture and apply the talents, energy and commitment of every team member. ZEEs are driven. ZEEs crave success. We tend to want things done one way. Our way. Invariably, we believe our way is the one right way, but something magical happens when we learn to delegate. We'll see successful outcomes, accomplished in ways different from our own, an experience that builds employee respect. Armed with this new success, you'll start interacting differently. Instead of browbeating and shaming your staff, instead of pointing out the fact that things weren't done the way you would have done them, you'll start talking with your staff and begin the process of discovering what's best—together.

Your job is simple.

Hire.

Train.

Trust.

Your challenge is to allow your staff to handle as much of the day-to-day operation as possible. Only then will you create the personal space you'll need to think about your growing business in new ways—to begin working on the business instead of working in the business.

As you consider your response, be honest with yourself. Are you really ready to turn over the reins?

5. Do you have the mental and emotional stamina you'll need to build a bigger business?

To answer this question, you must seriously consider if you're built for expansion. If you have a life partner or business partner (they may be the same person), you should have a serious and candid conversation about expansion and what it might mean to the business and to your relationship.

Reach out to close friends and trusted advisors like attorneys, bankers and accountants and share your plans (see Chapter 2: The TEMPO Effect, for a discussion of putting the power of TEMPO mindsets to work for you). Ask for candid feedback. Listen to understand how others view your ability to carry the weight of more responsibility and manage the emotional load of assuming more risk. If you've practiced the TEMPO mindsets, they'll know you are trying to find the answer that's right for you and are including them because the decision, whatever you decide, will impact them. You'll receive great feedback and demonstrate your commitment to mutual support for mutual success.

This activity is deceptively simple. Just a few questions to answer, easy-peasy. We've been conducting this exercise for a long time and know the longer you think about your response, the more deeply you consider the implications of each question, the more valuable your answers will be to you and to the other people you'll be explaining your decision to.

Before you begin writing out a response, read through and consider the commentary we've included below each question. In the age of computers, tablets and smartphones, it may seem easier and even more efficient to complete this activity digitally. We strongly suggest that you put aside the keyboard in favor of writing out your responses by hand. Yes, the process will take more time. Writing out your response longhand requires more effort. Rewriting your responses to make corrections and improve legibility is all part of a process designed to promote introspection and honest reflection. Hand writing your responses allows you to align the two most essential elements of your decision—your head and your heart.

Armed with a high-level understanding of your expansion options, the candid TEMPO feedback and your thoughtful responses to this exercise, you'll know if expansion is right for you.

SPOTLIGHT: THE COACH, KATIE YEARGAN

Athletes are not the only ones who benefit from great coaching. Everyone can learn from the hard-earned wisdom of a coach or mentor. Franchise operators are no exception. "The best franchise coaches tend to come from within the ranks of current and former operators. People like Jerry who know the franchise business inside and out and care deeply about helping other franchisees succeed," says Katie Yeargan.

Yeargan spent 18 years managing corporate-owned stores for some of the largest and most respected franchise systems. She then opened her own firm, providing consulting services for ZORs, ZEEs and people just thinking about getting into franchising. Her specialty? Helping businesses grow by cultivating their most valuable resource—talent. When asked why she became a franchise coach, she remarks simply, "I love the development of people."

Yeargan's passion reflects her belief that successful ZEEs need, "the passion and talent to run teams." If sheer numbers are any indication of her people passion, at one point Katie managed 550 salons with a roster of 65 regional executives. "Those stores were my stores, and those people were my people. A lot of the directors I worked with did not come up through the system like I did and that made it harder," she explains.

With the right coaching, many of the most common mistakes new ZEEs make can be avoided. "There's always a temptation to hire anyone, to just fill the slots you have to fill," she says. Katie has little patience for shortcuts. She believes, "creating something is much easier than recreating it. What happens is people get scared and just hire anyone and often they do not make the best players for what the team needs and those decisions last," she says, warning that if you're considering a franchise you need to be good at recruiting as well as understanding your industry to make sure you do it better than anyone else. Period.

"Recruiting and keeping good talent—people who will stay with you for years—employees who become more like family than worker bees, that is the goal you want to reach," she adds.

Katie advises ZEEs to be realistic about what it's going to take to build your business. "A lot of times, people really don't want to be hands-on business owners but an instant absentee owner. They want to set things up and get out quick and just cash the checks. Of course, you can earn that over time, but not at the beginning," Katie shares.

"They don't want to get calls on nights and weekends, but who is a stressed-out employee supposed to call instead?" The simple answer is it's your franchise and they're going to call you. After your team is in place, professionally trained, proven they can make tough decisions in your absence, then you can back off. And for those considering a franchise opportunity, "Ask the tough questions. Look at the worst-case scenario. Challenge all things. Don't be so excited that you don't go in with your eyes wide open. Know yourself and what you're passionate about. And take the time to get to know the business so you don't get into a business you're not excited about. And yes, listen to your coach, it can mean the difference between victory and defeat," Katie cautions.

Today Katie serves as vice president of development for a company focused on retail expansion, where she continues to put the lessons she's learned, and happily shares, into practice.

G2 SPECIAL EDITION

Young Entrepreneurs Present

FRANCHISE PROMOTION ROCK!

INCLUDES FUN WITH SUDS!

CHAPTER G2:
INVOLVING FAMILY

This chapter examines the question of family involvement in a franchise operation. In *Akers of Advice*, Jerry shares his views on the role of family and introduces a franchise phenomenon known as G2. The term G2 refers to an existing franchise operation run by a second-generation operator. The chapter then moves directly to a double-feature *Spotlight* that introduces Shelly Dorman and Sam Reges—Jerry's G2 daughters who have themselves become seasoned operators.

AKERS OF ADVICE: THE COMPANY OF FAMILY

Many ZEEs wonder if they should include family members in their new business. My answer is an unwavering, yes! For me, the opportunity to involve my family in building our franchise operation wasn't a question, it was a selling point. Long before I ever got serious about franchising, I had already envisioned my ideal work–life balance. I would bring my work into my personal life and bring my personal life into my work. But that's just the big family, farm boy in me talking. For others the decision is not so clear.

I know some of you just rolled your eyes at the prospect of going in to work, only to find it populated by the same people you just left at home. Not wanting to work with family is a totally understandable sentiment because spending every day and every night with your significant other might well put unnecessary strain on your relationship. Working with your grown kids holds similar challenges.

The decision you make isn't a statement about how much you love your family or how much you enjoy spending time with one another. It's a practical matter of shifting dynamics. Who's in charge at work? How will the new work roles affect interpersonal interactions at home? Consider also, the impact of not seeing your family while you are busy building your new business. A period that could last months or even years.

The decision that's right for you and your family is the decision that's right.

Period.

No judgement.

Do you sense the approach of a catch?

Is your Spidey-sense tingling?

Peter Parker would be proud, because the catch is this.

Formally including your family in the business is optional but (ah there it is) including your family in the business is not. If you opt for keeping business and family comfortably apart, you must do so with the understanding that the costs of building your business are not paid by you alone. Families foot the bill for the mood swings and the physical and psychological absences so common among new and expanding ZEEs. Families share the financial sacrifices often required during start-ups and downturns. Families need to know enough to understand when you need a shoulder to cry on and when you need a dance partner to celebrate with when good things happen. Even though your husband, wife or kids won't be working the cash register, it is your job to ensure that they feel engaged, involved (informally) and informed. Showing those you care about most that they have a role to play in your success, is a much better bet than excluding them.

Family can mean many things. By lineage or love or just landed at your door—family is what you say it is. When I talk about family here, I'm referring to the people in your life who matter most and not the hangers-on who inevitably appear with talk of jobs and paychecks. Engaging family doesn't mean that your paternal great-aunt's, dermatologist's simply-delightful-niece is somehow entitled to a paycheck just because you run the show.

There is no one universally right answer but there is only one right answer for you. Embrace the company-of-family in your family company or choose to take the helm on your own. The choice is yours.

SPOTLIGHT: THE MASCOT, SHELLY DORMAN

Shelly Dorman has always been a hard worker. At just ten-years-old, she was managing her own checking account and doing chores around the house and at her parents' business to earn money. Shelly quickly put her money to work, investing in livestock. She bottle-fed several calves into maturity and sold them for a tidy profit. Once she entered high school, Shelly and her sister Sam were recruited to work in the family franchise business.

"At 15, my first job was company mascot. I was the one in the costume. I was Suds, the living embodiment of a great shampoo. What could be better? Everyone loves a good hair wash and kids love to take baths.

Okay, it wasn't the greatest mascot idea, but all I had to do was wave to people at the hockey games. Easy, right? It wasn't! I was enclosed in this eight-foot shampoo bottle with huge clown feet, and I could barely see. I earned every penny of my pay," she says with a chuckle. Squeezing time in between typical teenage activities like sports and socializing, Shelly moved from special event management into day-to-day operations. First handling payroll, she convinced her parents to switch from manual bookkeeping to a new-fangled, computer-based system called QuickBooks. Catapulted into the digital age, the family business has never looked back. Today armed with a university degree in business management, Shelly is one of the managing partners of their operation sharing the role with her sister Sam. They are what's known in the franchise business as G2s, second-generation operators.

"When we started to get involved with our parents' salon, my sister and I never thought we'd have more than one store. Then we met another franchisee who wanted us to buy her salon, we did, and it just grew from there," says Shelly. They now own multiple locations. With that growth came more revenue and, of course, more expenses and headaches. But one thing that Shelly and her sister Sam learned from their parents—the value of a good employee.

"Taking care of people is our main job—first our employees, then our customers. You take care of them, treat them like family, give them a career path, a way to rise up in the organization and you'll build a dedicated team of loyal people who'll go the extra mile for you without asking," she explains. This strategy was handed down from their parents, but for Shelly it was mostly from her father. "My dad and I are both stubborn people. We clashed a lot when I was young. Now, we get each other and he trusts me with the day-to-day operations," she says, "He is also a solid businessperson, so much so that lots of smart people ask him for advice. The best advice he ever gave me was to take care of your most valuable business assets—your workers and yourself," Shelly continues.

She advises new franchisees to be realistic about the commitment necessary to become a successful operator. "When I'm on vacation, I get up before anyone else to check email or whatever means I have to stay in contact with my team and keep updated on open issues."

Interestingly, Shelly finds that her role at work mirrors the role she plays with her family outside of work. "Somewhere along the road, I fell into the role of middleman, just like at home. Always being in the middle of family disagreements and now disagreements between area managers and store employees suits me because I'm used to it. I don't get emotional." The ability to keep a cool head when the stress is high is a valuable skill for someone managing hundreds of people, and Shelly reports no shortage of opportunities to put that skill into action.

Shelly believes the odds for success are better when you operate a family business. "People come to us because we are family-run, it really matters to them. Even though we're a large company, it doesn't feel that way in any of our locations because each one has its own personality. My sister feels the same way. She knows the names and stories of every single staff member, in every location."

With her franchise future firmly in place, the big question is will there be a G3? A third generation one day operating the business. With younger children, Shelly admits that she has no idea what to expect. A glint in her eye suggests that she'd embrace the idea should it ever happen, adding, "Both of my kids were able to identify the company logo at an early age and it always brought a smile to their face. So, who knows?"

SPOTLIGHT: THE FRIEND, SAM REGES

Sam Reges is the kind of person who never met a stranger. That's a good thing because she and her sister have taken the reins of the family business—an operation that's all about customer love, loyalty and happy employees. Her family bought a franchise when she was in high school. Sam started working in the company from the early days and learned the operational side from the ground up.

"Without ever saying a word, our parents taught us the importance of treating customers and employees like family," says Sam. That's not just a cliché, but a strategy for making sure you earn customer loyalty and retain great employees. She learned that it's the little things that usually make that critical difference, like sitting with an elderly customer and showing her how to download their service app so she won't have to wait next time. The woman was thrilled, enjoying the care and attention.

Visibly moved, Sam offers another deeply personal example. "I remember seeing one of our employees sitting in the break room, anxious and gloomy. I learned that she had lost her apartment and had no place to go. I told her right off, we have to make sure you're taken care of and have a place to sleep tonight," recalls Sam, who then offered some suggestions and made some calls. The employee looked up at one point and remarked, "I'm grateful, but why do you care so much?" Sam was shocked and replied, "I don't understand why you'd even ask that. You're like family—we take care of family." Sam and another manager covered her shift so she could leave to find a new place. The employee was able to find a new apartment and put down a deposit using the salary advance Sam had given her. Because they took time to care, they helped change the ending to a story that could have turned out quite differently. "She's still with us today and she's thriving," Sam says, adding that kind of enthusiasm drives the entire business.

Sam cautions that working with family isn't always easy. "It's not always rainbows and unicorns—there are lots of challenges. I've always said the best thing about being in business with your family is you get to work with your family! And the worst thing about [being in] business with your family is—your family," she admits with a laugh. It's a double-edged sword as personality clashes that you thought were left at home spring up quickly.

"I don't live that close to our parents, but my sister does. Often, they tell her things or give some direction or even make some decision and forget to tell me," Sam shares. Communication is a common issue, one that many family-owned businesses contend with. As a young woman, Sam saw her parents' struggle. Married couples running a franchise, especially a chain, are often two ships passing in the night. "I'd say the key is simply this, set a time every single day to talk about what's going on, because if not you're going to miss each other and that causes friction," she advises.

Another issue Sam wants everyone considering a franchise to think about, especially with family ownership, is the myth of flexibility. "You are your own boss and that's one of the main reasons entrepreneurs and small business owners want it so badly. The reality is the ZEEs are servant leaders, always available to help when help is needed. I've been literally headed out the door for a night on-the-town, babysitter in place, engine running and ready to take that now-I-can-relax breath, when my cell phone rings," she says as if speaking about a specific memory. No matter how well you delegate, when crisis strikes, you get the call. "Dates get canceled, recitals go unseen and vacations get delayed. It's just the nature of the business," says Sam.

Sam and her sister found that the best way to minimize issues is to hire great people, give them great training and show you trust them by delegating as much of the day-to-day responsibilities as possible. In other words—getting and keeping great employees. "We offer good benefits, a retirement plan with a 401K, throwing appreciation parties and any excuse we can find to let our employees know how much we owe our success to them. My parents' philosophy was to treat them as family and once they know we mean it, they go the extra mile for us. And someday, they'll do the same for Sam's and my children, too." she says with a hint of pride.

LIFT

GIANT
LEAP

ZEE

ONE SMALL STEP

FROM ME TO ZEE
IMPOSSIBLE TRANSITION?

IN DEPTH:

WORST IN TRAVEL
AWARD COVERAGE

CHAPTER 14:
ONE SMALL STEP

fter I completed the *Live It 2 Own It* manuscript, I surprised my wife Sheila with a trip to celebrate her birthday. It was a big round-number birthday that called for special attention. While I've traveled extensively for work, we'd never really had the chance to travel together (read as, *without kids*) and it was starting to feel like we never would. We weren't able to take a honeymoon when we got married and when the kids were younger, family vacations were happily our focus.

When our nest began to empty, Sheila and I decided to take the *just-us* plunge. We booked a once-in-a-lifetime cruise. As the sailing drew closer, we learned that some 3,600 people, all passengers and crew of the Diamond Princess cruise liner, were being quarantined because of something called COVID-19.

I remember thinking, "what's COVID-19?"

The answer to that question changed the world. At the time, all we knew for sure was that as amateur travel agents, my wife and I were a bust. If there was a game show for ill-timed travel plans, we'd win hands down because we'd created a vacation that was so wrong for the moment, so deeply misaligned with the unfolding state of the world, that every element of the itinerary, taken independently, topped its own list of worst choices. I could hear the game show host in my head. "What is *the* riskiest way to travel in the world today? You picked cruising. Survey says...*cruising*. [Ding!] Number one answer. Nicely done. Now, on to the bonus round. What three travel destinations must travelers avoid most right now?"

"Well, my wife and I picked Spain, France and Italy. How'd we do?" I'd reply.

"You've done it! You hit the bad travel trifecta, your itinerary included not one, but all three of the destinations that travelers need to avoid most. Congratulations, you've won immediate trip cancellation!"

Of course, our experience was inconsequential, insignificant in comparison to the devastation COVID-19 wrought. We were very lucky. We know and appreciate that fact. The point of this story lies below its surface. It's subtle, and all too common.

Even before the cruise fiasco, we'd already had the feeling that *just-us* travel wasn't in the cards and this was just the universe reinforcing the message. Except it wasn't. We'd allowed ourselves to accept a narrative about who we were and what we could and could not do. It's all too common, and there's no better example of the phenomena than the transition from worker to independent business owner.

For 25 years, Jerry was caught in a loop of his own making. A loop that kept him from taking the one step that would move him from analysis to action, from an old daydream to new day job. I don't believe that Jerry was unable to find a suitable franchise option in all that time and neither does he. Something else was at work. It was that same something that keeps us from getting up off the couch and going to the gym, that same something that surrenders diets, keeps us from learning another language, ensures we never learn to play an instrument, draw a masterpiece or sing at

Carnegie Hall. I know what it is, and I've given it a name—*fear of future self.*

Like the old saying, *better the devil you know than the devil you don't,* we dream of becoming better versions of ourselves—better, faster, stronger. We are motivated, dedicated and consistent in our desire but few of us ever realize our better selves. Why? Because, for better or worse, we are who we are today. For better or worse, we've figured out how to survive at being what we are right now. To change, even change for the better, means facing the unknown and the unknown is risky, the unknown is scary. Like being granted three wishes by an untrustworthy genie or making a deal with the devil, we fear becoming our future self comes with hidden costs, costs which are much too high. We fear that one day the fondest hope of our future self will be to return to the safety and security of the self we are right now.

If you've read the book and decided that franchising isn't for you, you've succeeded. The book did its job of helping you along your journey and you did the work to find your truth—well done!

If you've read the book and believe that a career in franchising is what you want, you now face your own *fear of future self* challenge. Before you leave these pages. Before you go back to your daily grind and run the risk of falling into your own unproductive loop, you owe it to yourself (both your current self and your future self) to transform your desire into tangible action.

If you didn't complete the chapter activities as you read, complete them now or get a copy of the *Live It 2 Own It Activities* Workbook to help organize your work and keep it all in one place.

If you've done the work and have already narrowed your search to a few high potential franchise models, reach out to these franchise representatives and start the conversations.

If you are serious about franchising right now, the time to act is now.

If your life is hectic and you plan to get to it soon, chances are you won't.

What's holding you back? What are you really afraid of?

Answer honestly and you'll be on your way to breaking the cycle before it begins.

POSTSCRIPT—WHEN THE DAY FINALLY CAME

I've logged well over 1,000,000 miles in the air, but I'd never been happier to board a plane. Happy not just because my wife's big-round-birthday surprise unfolded as planned but because it felt like a spell had been broken. One small step for us, one giant step in how we saw ourselves and our future.

In one small step we came to grips with our unspoken fears. We feared that reconnecting with one another might somehow mean being less connected with our children. We feared the guilt we'd feel at putting ourselves first after two kids-first decades. And we feared that the entire process meant we were getting older and all that entailed. All it took was one small step to generate one giant leap in our perspective and put our fears to rest.

Now, go take that step!

It's time for you to *Live It 2 Own It...*

AFTERWORD:
ROB GOGGINS, GREAT CLIPS PRESIDENT

Twenty years ago, my wife Katie and I signed up to become franchisees with a national franchise chain. We completed the paperwork, wrote a big check, and quickly came to the realization that we had selected the wrong partners. The business never opened.

It was a low point, personally and professionally. An expensive lesson that meant my franchise career ended before it began—at least that's what my wife and everyone around us thought.

In a world populated by talented women and men dedicated to building sustainably successful businesses across the globe, our first franchise experience was a rare exception. Still, every new business owner, franchisee or not, must navigate the often-rocky terrain of the business start-up. I see it every day: determined operators, growing and learning, stumbling and sometimes failing, as they move from novice newcomer to operations master.

Katie and I paid a remarkably high price for our mistake. We lost money we could not afford to lose. There were mental and emotional costs as well. Surely, the experience was more than enough justification for me to turn my back on the franchising model forever.

Why didn't I just walk away from the industry?

It took a long time and lots of self-searching before I could answer that question. The experience had certainly changed me, but it did not change my belief in people, a belief in the limitless possibilities that exist when good people come together to create something bigger than themselves. A belief that is so ingrained in the franchising model, it's not really all that surprising that I ended up right back where I'd started.

A little older and a little wiser, I purposefully aligned myself with companies and people with strong values and a commitment to helping others reach their goals. The years have only strengthened my resolve. The whole concept of helping people achieve their dreams and building the systems and processes to achieve them, just feels right to me.

Today, I have the privilege of serving as President of Great Clips, a franchise system that started, and remains, a family-owned business. Every day I do my best to lead by example and work to help us answer the questions that matter most. How do we hire, develop, and reward the right people? How do we bring the right franchisees on board? How do we give back to our respective communities and live up to our corporate responsibility to help build a better world? How do we achieve our goals and our vision?

In 2022, Great Clips will celebrate 40 years of operation. In that short time, the system has grown to include more than 4,400 units in 190 markets, serving some two million customers a week – making Great Clips the world's largest salon brand. Our vision is: Working together to build the most profitable salons by delivering the most powerful and enduring brand. Executing that vision resulted in Entrepreneur magazine ranking Great Clips the #1 brand in its category and #13 overall on its Franchise

500 list. The ranking reflects value for costs and fees, franchisee support, financial strength and stability, size and growth, as well as overall strength of brand.

We owe much of our success to the quality of our operators. We continuously look for franchisees who are willing and able to follow our system. We evaluate franchise candidates in terms of how well we think they'll work with our team, cooperate with other franchisees and collaborate with local market partners and vendors. That's why I'm so excited about *Live It 2 Own It*. The book guides prospective franchisees through every step of the franchise journey. From conducting smarter searches (a real time saver), to teaching would-be franchisees how to interview franchisors as they would a potential employee. From hiring and staffing, to opening day and expansion, the book offers practical and tactical advice to ensure the important questions don't go unasked, or worse – unanswered!

In the book, Jerry talks about why it took him 25 years to pick a franchise, a process that would have been far shorter if he'd had *Live It 2 Own It* as his guide. He would have known to read franchise disclosure documents to quickly narrow his search. He would have known to talk to as many people as possible in the system, and people that left the system, to understand how it all works – or why it doesn't. Even though *Live it 2 Own It* didn't exist back then, we are fortunate that Jerry found his way to Great Clips as we ended up with a great owner-operator.

Jerry, his wife Mickey, and now their daughters Sam and Shelly are like many Great Clips franchisees, they want to give back. With a successful business that's seamlessly transitioned to a second-generation operation, they don't have to be asked to help others, they seek out opportunities to do so. Jerry helps other franchisees and sits on the International Franchise

Association board and the Iowa Board of Cosmetology Arts & Sciences. He conducts staff training that goes well beyond haircuts and how to provide the five steps of customer service. He helps stylists learn what they need to know to purchase their first home or car. He shows them how to create and manage a budget if that's what they need. That's the level of care that is truly people-first.

It's hard to believe, but I've been with Great Clips in one capacity or another for nearly 15 years and I'm still as excited and full of energy as I was on day one. I do whatever I can to stay connected to the real people that make up our brand and do the real work of making our customers happy. Every quarter or so, I visit one of our salons, work reception for several hours, greet customers, talk to the stylists, clean shelves, fold towels, sweep the floor, the things we expect stylists to do every day.

Along with our more than 1,100 franchisees across the United States and Canada, Jerry and his family embody the qualities we seek in franchisees who wish to join the Great Clips brand. People who roll up their sleeves every day to build their local business, one customer and one employee at a time. This is what I've always admired about franchising: franchisees working together with the franchisor to build something bigger than either could have done on their own. With *Live It 2 Own It*, prospective franchisees now have a friendly voice, offering solid advice, every step of the way as they seek to find that same franchise fit to help them achieve their goals and dreams. I finally found my home with Great Clips, and I hope you utilize the advice in this book to help you find the right franchise home for you and your family.

-Rob Goggins

ACKNOWLEDGEMENTS

Books transmit and transform. *Good* books are the work of a community of people bound by a commitment to the care and feeding of an idea. *Great* books help us think differently, work differently and get things done. From *good* to *great*, *Live It 2 Own It* is what you, the reader, make of it—but the quality of the team who created this book is without question.

Dedicated to helping readers like you, the team worked even when no one was looking, freely surrendered nights and weekends without ever being asked. Reflecting the shape of the emerging rapid response organizational design, our team includes a mix of full-time staff and a broad community of specialist contractors (people with whom we work so closely and so often that the distinction's lost meaning), all supported by a growing legion of contributions ready to help change our relationship with work.

From the day a hairstylist named Deidre Layfield insisted I meet a man named Jerry Akers to the moment we completed the final track of the audiobook, *Live It 2 Own It* has been about a growing cast of individuals, each contributing in unique and invaluable ways. At the center of all the action, Chief of Staff, Alyssa Nolte lived the L20 philosophy every day. No matter the weight of task or the number of impossible missions she took on, Alyssa continuously exhibited the rarest mix of raw talent, unbridled enthusiasm and seemingly limitless energy. Our team added a whole new dimension with the addition of Tara Thomas-Gettman, the longtime nightly news anchor turned communications executive, who leads our editorial team, which included educational editor Kelly Fagan, screenwriter and copy editor Greg Perkins, our own next gen super talent Emily Hammer and manuscript reviewer Dorothy Bates.

Our deepest appreciation goes to the people that brought our words to life, including our publishing and graphic arts team headed by Susan Langman. Joe Hox, the extraordinarily talented artist that transformed L2O into original chapter art. Mike Carlo and his amazing audio and production team led by Deb Niermann, Brendon Hagarty and Scott Braun. Jim and Becky Mudd and everyone in the Mudd Advertising family, you've been great partners and amazing friends every step of the way.

Special thanks to our executive sponsors Steve Reasner and Paul Bernstein at LIFTventures and the entire staff of LIFTinnovate, led by Jennifer Naylor, the best operations and HR executive in the business.

For one last acknowledgement, I return to the beginning.

Two desks, two chairs and just two people.

Thank you, Amber Moore, for always taking my crazy ideas seriously.

Look what we're building now!

GLOSSARY

Brand consistency	Remaining true to the brand guidelines the franchisor sets forth for franchisees
Business health checks	Consistent efforts to evaluate the state of your business to identify early warning signs of failure and stop them before they become more serious issues
Churn	The natural turnover of employees in a business
Commercial viability	Ensuring that a business, product, or service will be able to compete effectively and make a profit
Cost	Your initial franchise investment limit to narrow down the number of relevant results *(Related to: SORT Method)*
Cost of operation	What you can expect to spend to start the business, ongoing fees, and day-to-day operational expenditures *(Related to: Rank-and-Test Criteria)*
D.I.Y. real estate team	A group of local real-estate agents and brokers who a franchisee builds a personal relationship with to leverage their expertise of the local market
Diversification	Expansion focusing on operating multiple units of multiple brands in the same or differing geographies *(Related to: Expansion)*
Effective time management	A subset of the Time mindset valuing production and getting things done *(Related to: TEMPO)*
Efficient time management	A subset of the Time mindset valuing prioritization and getting the right things done *(Related to: TEMPO)*
Employer of choice	A place where potential candidates are heavily drawn to and people desire to work

Employment party	A staffing tactic to attract potential applicants by inviting candidates to learn more about your business opportunities in a social setting *(Related to: Staffing promotion plan)*
Expansion	Growing your franchise business by opening new locations *(Related to: Expansion)*
Expertise mindset	Valuing expertise as a high-value resource by developing new skills and specialized knowledge and tapping into the expertise of others *(Related to: TEMPO)*
Fast growth	The speed of adoption by the community in response to the previously unaddressed need or niche *(Related to: Rank-and-Test Criteria)*
Franchise advisor	An impartial specialist who works with potential franchisees to objectively evaluate an opportunity and the franchisor's reputation
Franchise advisory council	A group of people elected or appointed to advise a franchisor on decisions regarding franchising and provide franchisees a platform to deliver feedback
Franchise associations	Groups that provide small business services and other resources to franchisees
Franchise coach	An impartial specialist who works with franchisees to address early warning signs of failure, course correct to avoid failure, and achieve desired results
Franchise training	The process and resources that exposes franchisees to many of the functions necessary to run the business
FUD	Fear, uncertainty, and doubt as a collection of mental states that may influence your thinking

G2	An existing franchise operation run by a second-generation operator
Geography	Including the geography where you would like to open a franchise to narrow down the number of relevant results *(Related to: SORT Method)*
GO plan	A campaign detailing the promotional activities used to support the grand opening of your new business
Home budgeting training	Basic financial planning in hopes the experience will make the employee more successful and stable in their career *(Related to: Training)*
Home-based or mobile	Choosing between running the business from your own home, travelling to operate your business, or opening a traditional store front location *(Related to: Rank-and-Test Criteria)*
Industry type	The different types of business activities, models, and customer experiences *(Related to: Rank-and-Test Criteria)*
Initial evaluation criteria	Standards that reflect your priorities by which you evaluate franchise opportunities and decide which franchise is right for you
Initial Investment (Price)	The total amount necessary to begin franchise operations *(Related to: Rank-and-Test Criteria)*
Inorganic expansion	Expansion focusing on riskier growth with potentially very high returns that provides instant gratification and is measured by the rate of business output growth *(Related to: Expansion)*
Jackpot thinking	A thought process that favors large payouts and flawed reasoning that neglects practicality and ignores risks

Keyword	A specific term that reflects your desires for a franchise opportunity and can be used to narrow down the number of relevant results *(Related to: SORT Method)*
Leverage model	A type of inorganic expansion that leverages cash generated by profitable units to cover the shortfall of launching a new location *(Related to: Expansion)*
Local market flexibility	Decisions that the franchisor decides are best left to the franchisee
Management training	Building a pipeline of management prospects to fill out your executive team and support future growth opportunities *(Related to: Training)*
Marketing mix	The set of tools and customer strategy used to meet the market needs you've identified regarding price, product, place, and promotion
Mid-year analysis	Examination of annual goals with respect to your half-year performance
Mindset	A set of assumptions, methods, or notions that affect your ability to capitalize on opportunities and overcome challenges *(Related to: TEMPO)*
Money mindset	Valuing money as a high-value resource by seeking to get a disproportionate amount of value out of every dollar and dig deeper into the value equation *(Related to: TEMPO)*
New or existing	Choosing between buying an existing franchise unit or opening a brand-new location *(Related to: Rank-and-Test Criteria)*
Operational excellence	Continued efforts to reinvigorate the business by establishing and communicating an operational agenda and goals leading to top 10% performance

Opportunity mindset
Valuing opportunities as a high-value resource by seeking out opportunities that others do not and and leveraging opportunities for more value
(Related to: TEMPO)

Organic expansion
Expansion focusing on safer growth with smaller, incremental results from improvement to existing business operations
(Related to: Expansion)

Organize opportunities
The second step of the SORT method which orders franchise opportunities into manageable lists to stay organized throughout the process and prepare for review and analysis
(Related to: SORT Method)

Owner role
How active the franchisor expects the franchisee to be in day-to-day operations
(Related to: Rank-and-Test Criteria)

Passive investor
A type of franchisee who seeks to turn the reins of their franchise over to others and shows up occasionally to collect their profits

Peaks
Period of time during your business's hours of operations where there is an increase in the number of customers

People mindset
Valuing people as a high-value resource by aligning your own people with other people's people for mutual benefit
(Related to: TEMPO)

People-powered business
A mindset that focuses on treating employees with respect and making connections with them

Poaching
Engaging with staff of other local businesses with the intent of enticing them away from their current place employment to join your team

Professional money	Private equity injected into franchise systems that focuses on short-term profit yield at the expense of long-term growth
Promotional mix	The promotional options and tactical plan you select to achieve your business objectives and execute the marketing strategy
Rank & Test	The third step of the SORT method which uses your goals and objectives to evaluate potential franchise opportunities and reduce your search to the most relevant options *(Related to: SORT Method)*
Relationship building & networking training	Making connections that bind customers to your business on a personal level and allow them to become an extended member of the business family *(Related to: Training)*
Relationship development training	Treating customers with respect and make continued efforts to connect with them *(Related to: Training)*
Renegotiation strategy	A tactic to approach the property owner to renew your lease and potentially negotiate a lower lease rate
Renewal process	Steps taken at the end of the franchise agreement to renew the license and allow the franchisee to continue operating their franchise
Search smart	The first step of the SORT method which employs enhanced search capabilities to focus your search efforts on relevant franchise opportunities *(Related to: SORT Method)*
Search string	Combining keywords to narrow the number of relevant results further than the power of just one keyword *(Related to: SORT Method)*

Single unit, territory or geography	Choosing between owning a single unit or managing several other locations within a territory or geography *(Related to: Rank-and-Test Criteria)*
Site selection	The joint process between a franchisee and their franchisor of selecting a commercial property for the franchise
Soft opening	Opening the franchise to a select, invited group of people before the grand opening to practice for the upcoming grand opening and identify areas for improvement
SORT method	A method of conducting a productive franchise opportunity search *(Search, Organize, Rank & Test)*
Staffing promotion plan	A media tactic designed to effectively attract desirable candidates for staffing to a business
Storyselling	A businessperson's ability to tell the human stories that underpin business activity
Table stakes	The minimum requirements to reasonably enter the franchise game, including mastering the facts and making the case for commercial viability
TEMPO Effect	Positioning yourself to accelerate business development, increase decision quality, and secure resources by employing TEMPO mindsets *(Time, Expertise, Money, People, Opportunities)*
The Dirty Dozen	An initial list of 12 potential franchises that come to mind *(Related to: SORT Method)*
Time mindset	Valuing time as a high-value resource by seeking to get the most out of every minute of the day and focusing on what is really important *(Related to: TEMPO)*

Timeout	Designated time to review the business, analyze progress, and modify any plans and strategies to improve operations
Training	Programs that strengthen your operation, enhance employee skills, and build leadership bench strength through employee preparation
Value based sales training	Finding ways of benefiting customers throughout a sale by guiding them through the sales process and helping them make an informed decision *(Related to: Training)*
ZEEs	The nickname given to franchisees
ZORs	The nickname given to franchisors
ZOR-ZEE relationship	The interdependent, mutually accountable relationship between a franchisor and a franchisee

Live It 2 Own It is just the beginning...

To continue the journey and find out more about how you can tell
your franchise story and be a part of our next book, please visit
www.LiveIt2OwnIt.com

Made in the USA
Columbia, SC
15 February 2022

55924132R00180